WAR, PEACE, and
RECONCILIATION

WAR, PEACE, and RECONCILIATION

A Theological Inquiry

Theodore R. Weber

CASCADE Books • Eugene, Oregon

WAR, PEACE, AND RECONCILIATION
A Theological Inquiry

Copyright © 2015 Theodore R. Weber. All rights reserved. Except for brief quotations in critical publications or reviews, no part of this book may be reproduced in any manner without prior written permission from the publisher. Write: Permissions, Wipf and Stock Publishers, 199 W. 8th Ave., Suite 3, Eugene, OR 97401.

Cascade Books
An Imprint of Wipf and Stock Publishers
199 W. 8th Ave., Suite 3
Eugene, OR 97401

www.wipfandstock.com

ISBN 13: 978-1-4982-1855-9

Cataloging-in-Publication data:

Weber, Theodore R.

    War, peace, and reconciliation : a theological inquiry / Theodore R. Weber.

    x + 172 p. ; 23 cm. —Includes bibliographical references and index.

    ISBN 13: 978-1-4982-1855-9

    1. War—Religious aspects. 2. Reconciliation—Religious aspects. I. Title.

BT736.2 .W43 2015

Manufactured in the U.S.A.

*To my friends and colleagues of the Candler "Young Turks,"
who endured to become the "Old Guard":*

Hendrik Boers
Manfred Hoffmann
William Mallard
Theodore Runyon

Contents

Acknowledgments ix

1. The Problem: How to Think as Christians about War and Peace 1
2. War and Reconciliation: Logics and Contexts 16

PART ONE: *The Theological Context*

3. The History of Divine Grace: The Context of Reconciliation 27
4. Fundamental Reality and Its Disruptions 37
5. Judgment, Preservation, and Historical Preservation 45

PART TWO: *The Political Context*

6. War in the Context of Politics 69
7. The Meanings and Problems of Power 81
8. The Civilizing of Power 89
9. The International System, and Other Matters 101

PART THREE: *Peace, Justice, the Church*

10. Peace: The Freedom to Be Vulnerable 121
11. Justice, Power, and Peace 133
12. Rethinking the "Just War Ethic" 140
13. Reconciliation, War, and the Church 147

Concluding Reflections 159
Bibliography 161
Index 165

Acknowledgments

This book was written with the support of The Alfred Heilbrun Distinguished Research Fellowship for Emory Emeritus Faculty in Arts and Sciences, named in honor of Alfred B. Heilbrun Jr., Professor Emeritus of Psychology. I want to thank the Heilbrun family for providing the funding for this fellowship, and the Emeritus College of Emory University for granting it. The book itself results from years of reflection on the relationship of Christian theology, ethics, and international politics. Numerous persons and groups have encouraged and challenged my thinking on this relationship across the years. Preeminent, especially in earlier years, was the forum provided by the Council on Religion and International Affairs, whose president was A. William Loos. Also, across the years I have benefited greatly from scholarly discussion with a number of persons of similar interests, especially Paul Ramsey, Alan Geyer, William V. O'Brien, Quentin Quade, and Glenn Stassen, all of whom—sadly—are now deceased. William Mallard read an early draft of the work and offered validating commentary on my use of St. Augustine. Stacy Hood and Rob Weber provided invaluable assistance in preparing the manuscript for typesetting. Numerous students in the Candler School of Theology and the Laney Graduate School of Arts and Sciences supplied fora for the presentation of these ideas and prodded my conceptual understanding. No statement of this kind would be complete without acknowledging the love and support of my wife, Mudie, throughout the sixty years of our marriage.

1

The Problem: How to Think as Christians about War and Peace

It is fun and inspiring to sing, "Ain't gonna study war no more!" Regrettably it is no kind of guidance for Christian responsibility in the world. Christians are called to work for peace. To do that they must "study war"—not in order to make war, but to find out why it occurs and to learn how to bring its motives and energies under control. But first of all, to study war and peace they must discern the contours of reality disclosed by their Christian faith, and with that theological understanding begin to investigate the demands and challenges of war and the promises of peace. Note the order: First, establish the theological method and context. Second, armed with that knowledge make the inquiry into the political setting and historical occasion of war. That combination will constitute the study of war—and demonstrate the paths to and prospects for peace.

A study of that sort was the idea supporting an international, indeed intercontinental, conference titled "Theology, Politics, and Peace," held at Emory University and the Carter Presidential Center in Atlanta, Georgia, in April 1988. The focus of the conference was a critical interaction among three Christian approaches to political understanding and peacemaking, each of them highly influential, and each originating on a different continent. Professor Jürgen Moltmann represented German political theology, Professor José Míguez Bonino spoke for Latin American liberation theology, and I was asked to interpret the American tradition of Christian Realism in relation to the other two positions.[1]

[1]. The three addresses, along with numerous other submissions, were published in Runyon, *Theology, Politics, and Peace*. My address is titled "Christian Realism, Power, and Peace," 55–76.

The choice of political theology and liberation theology, and of their two representatives, was self-evident, given the contemporary prominence and influence both of the movements themselves and of their eminent and distinguished spokespersons. The inclusion of the American tradition of Christian Realism in a conversation with German political theology and Latin American liberation theology raised some eyebrows, mainly because many adherents of these other positions see it—whether rightly or wrongly—as an ideological defender of the entrenched powers of which they are strenuous critics. For them, Reinhold Niebuhr is more likely the enemy than a theological ally. Nevertheless, the inclusion of this third position required no justification. Niebuhr's Christian Realism directly and substantively engages the problems of war and peacemaking, and does so from a Christian theological stance. It is an older theopolitical tradition than the other two. Míguez Bonino studied at Union Theological Seminary in New York when Reinhold Niebuhr was a faculty member there, and Moltmann reported that the first book he read of (what he called) "dogmatic theology" was Niebuhr's *Nature and Destiny of Man*.[2] Niebuhrian realism continues as a potent intellectual and political force even today. Presidents Carter and Obama, among many others prominent in American politics and journalism, have been and are readers of Niebuhr. Theologians with profound objections to some aspects of Niebuhr's thought find that they must wrestle with him, and not simply ignore him. Hence the necessity and authenticity of including Christian Realism in the conversation.[3]

---

2. Moltmann's recollection was offered in personal conversations and public settings, as well as in published statements. When I asked him to say more about his early reading of Niebuhr, he replied, "But I've forgotten that." I doubt it, although Niebuhr certainly was not formative for his thinking.

3. My own role as the position's spokesperson required some qualification. In my opening remarks I noted that I stood in quite a different relation to the position I was representing from the other two speakers. Both of them were prominent originators of their theological traditions, who not only represented their theologies but shaped them as they spoke. By contrast, I had entered the theological culture of Christian Realism after it had been originated by Reinhold Niebuhr and been developed by him and by others, including Paul Ramsey. I saw myself as a "later generation" entry, one who was old enough to have heard Niebuhr preach and lecture, had for several decades taught a course titled "The Thought of Reinhold Niebuhr," and was a friend (but not a disciple) of Paul Ramsey, but who engaged Christian Realism mainly by reflecting and improvising on what the creative predecessors had done. In other words, I did not have the same authority of representing a theological tradition as did my two distinguished colleagues. Nor could I consider myself a "Christian Realist" in an exclusive and definitive sense. I was convinced, for the most part, by Niebuhr's understanding of the ambiguity of human

However, this book is not a defense of Reinhold Niebuhr and Christian Realism, nor is it a continuing analysis and critique of the other positions represented. It is an exploration of the theology of reconciliation, showing how even war, with its massive destruction and unrelenting cruelty, is a proper object of reconciling ministry, and how the theology itself is developed and illuminated by this engagement. It expounds and demonstrates a particular Christian theological stance. It includes also a substantive investigation of the political context of war, of power as substantial and relational, of peace as an organization of power, of the historic transition from a European state system to a genuinely *international* system. As I stated earlier, first the theology, then the political analysis, with both essential in combination in any Christian thinking about war and peace. In these respects it remains within the purpose of the conference, which was to consider the interrelationships of theology, politics, and peace.

Preliminary Observations on Reconciliation

In a subsequent chapter I shall explore the meanings of reconciliation more fully. Here I want to offer some preliminary thoughts on what it is and is not. Reconciliation in the fundamental theological sense employed in this book is God's work—the movement of divine grace through history, engaging all the aspects of brokenness and promise, and reaching its climax of fulfillment and disclosure in the life, death, and resurrection of Jesus Christ. It is the renewal of the fallen creation according to its original divine intention, the recovery of the human purpose of imaging God in caring for God's creation, and of working cooperatively in doing so. With this grand coverage it includes the conflicts of nations, which are aspects of the fallen creation and manifestations of its disruption.

Reconciliation, explained thusly, is in its initiative and history God's work, not primarily and essentially a human work. Nevertheless, it is also—and in consequence—a human work. Just as human beings were created by God to "care for the garden," so too are they called by God to share in the work of recovering and renewing the same garden disrupted and spoiled by

---

nature, the limits of historical expectation, the necessity for love to seek justice for the neighbor and to use power in doing so, and the fragmentary character and tentativity of any concrete achievements of justice. However, my approach was and is more directly christological than Niebuhr's, and my method of thinking about life in general and politics in particular is more inferential from the reconciling history of the work of God.

human sin. The special work of Christians is to disclose the existence and the power of this process, and to share in it. In point of faith, they know that in following their calling they are grounded and guided in this gracious history of God. Just what kind and degree of reconciliation they can achieve are problems to be worked through in this book.

At this point, let us attempt some further clarifications. First, reconciliation is a corporate concept before it is an individualistic or interpersonal concept. Primarily that is because God's work of healing and recovery is for the whole of the fallen creation, not just for individual persons or their fractured relationships. In both its divine and human dimensions it is a community-building enterprise, striving toward the realization of what Martin Luther King Jr. called "the beloved community." But also it recognizes the social nature of human beings—they are persons emergent and embedded in social institutions and groups, and often defined by them. Those who reach out to each other from divergent social locations never are fully empowered to be reconciled until the effects of these societal barriers are overcome. Hence the necessity of defining reconciliation primarily (but not exclusively) in terms of societal transformation and inclusiveness.

Second, theologically guided reconciliation is a matter of contextual discernment, not of method. Methods of encounter and transformation certainly are important, but they are not fundamental to the vocation of reconciliation. When Saddam Hussein invaded Kuwait in 1990 and threatened Saudi Arabia, the United States and its gathered allies made plans to expel the Iraqis by military force. At that time, a group of persons of Christian inspiration offered a counterproposal: "Let us try reconciliation," they urged, "not war." I had serious doubts as to the adequacy of their political analysis, but I was troubled even more by their theology. Their proposal was to *try reconciliation*, which implied that reconciliation is a technique or procedure—presumably nonviolent—that holds unusual promise of greater effectiveness in resolving the conflict in a truly constructive and healing manner, but is not yet recognized for its relevance to the problem being addressed by material and damaging forms of power. Viewed thusly, reconciliation is a sometime thing, a religious "specialty," left out of usual deliberations and brought in only when things get really bad—and seem probably hopeless. Moreover, given this understanding, it is the specifically *Christian* way to engage the threatening and destructive realities of war.

I contend, however, for the relationship of reconciliation to war as that of a context of discernment, not that of a special and superior method of resolution. The context is the comprehensive working of divine grace to overcome the disruptions in human society, and especially the disruptive, destructive, and idolatrous phenomenon of military struggle. What is discerned in the primary sense is the working of grace to set the struggle on the road to healing and wholeness—to the recovery of human reality as the divine image and of human vocation in a corporate sense as the common stewardship of the earth. This discernment of grace discloses the ways in which political analysis and reorganization serve the divine purposes, however meagerly and reluctantly. And yet the very same discernment in the context of grace discloses that human efforts toward peace, though important and helpful, always fall short of the divine plan and expectation. The maximum human beings can achieve in their temporal work of reconciliation is to develop a society in which the members are relatively free to be vulnerable. That is a lot, but it is much less than the kingdom of God, and it is much more fragile.

Third, reconciliation in international conflict, as in other arenas, is a process, not a goal. The setting of particular goals often is important and necessary, but to define reconciliation as an end-goal, an ideal relegated to a far-off future, makes it something that can be set aside as remote and irrelevant. Reconciliation is a present and a constant activity, something to be worked at in every moment and situation. It is a call to enter a process, to transcend immediate realities of alienation, and to do so in response to the grace of God pressing toward wholeness. It is the work at hand. This work will be a demand of grace so long as sin is present in human experience.

Other Possible Approaches

My decision to focus on the reconciling work of God as the governing concept in this process of thinking about war means that I have not chosen some other approaches that are prominent, and at times dominant, in this kind of discussion.

Renouncing Violence, and "Following Jesus"

Specifically, I have not made renunciation of violence the touchstone for Christian thinking about war. When viewed in the context of the history of gracious renewal, violence is something to be subdued and controlled, not something simply to be renounced. Implicit in what I have said is a decidedly negative attitude toward violence, because it is prime evidence of the disruption of the divine plan; however, one should not therefore abstract it from the total fabric of ruination and resistance with which divine reconciliation must work. The starting point for Christian thinking about war is the work of God in bringing the fallen creation to the realization of wholeness, healing, and development. How to deal with violence falls within the context of that work, but it is not the starting point for faith and action. With regard to nonviolent resistance or direct action, there are times when that commitment is the correct situational expression of Christian vocation, but it is not the definition of Christian response as such.

The decision to renounce violence on principle follows often from the decision to make "following Jesus" the basis for Christian discipleship generally and war-thinking in particular.[4] In no way do I dismiss the authority and relevance of the Jesus of the Gospels. Much of what Jesus did and said are timeless directives for the message and activity of the church. Jesus is Lord and Savior. The fundamental theological relevance of Jesus of Nazareth is that he is both climax and essential instrument of the plan of God to redeem and revitalize the fallen creation—that is the christological construal of "following Jesus." It is not his role as moral teacher or his statements or stance on any given issue, or even his nonviolent acceptance of the cross. What is the plan of God, and what is the role of Jesus in the plan? That is the primary focus for Christian understanding—not his attitudes toward violence.

The immediate difficulty in "following Jesus" with regard to violence and related matters is that the political situation confronting him was not war but rebellion and revolution. The Gospel setting is the prospect of replacing Roman rule with the kingdom of God. The Zealots are prepared and eager to use violence to effect the transformation, and expect fully that they will receive divine assistance. In that setting Jesus rejects the use of violence emphatically, because the purpose of using it then and there was to bring in the kingdom of God. In his view, the kingdom will come in God's own time and by God's efforts. It cannot be established by violent

---

4. A popular approach to guidance for Christian action on tough questions is to ask, "What would Jesus do?" The implication is that Jesus is a non-historical sage who can be lifted out of his own context and expected to speak authoritatively to problems he could not have imagined. If we are going to ask what would Jesus do about basic issues of contemporary international politics, we must lift him out of his own Roman-Jewish situation and plop him down in the office of president or secretary of State. That would be more than a minor exercise in historical wrenching and messianic transformation.

men using violent methods. That is the historical context in which Jesus addresses the issue of violence. He does not deal with the issue in general and abstractly.

His rejection of violent means is applicable to war, but specifically to those wars that are put forth as means to redeem history by military conquest, that is, to establish a secular (or religious) equivalent of the kingdom of God. Violence will not bring in God's kingdom. At best, it will rearrange the material conditions of human society. Perhaps the rearrangement will improve things, but no political reordering—especially any engineered with military force—will bring a messianic end to the internal contradictions of human history.

However, if war is an instrument in the divine work of preservation in a world wracked by sin, it has a different rationale. In that case one must raise the basic questions of justification for war. But even those questions are to be addressed within the history of the divine work of redemption, and not as problems of following Jesus. The fundamental concern in redemptive history is neither the flat rejection of uses of coercive force nor their legitimation, but the recognition that uses of force are present and active in a fallen world and must be brought increasingly under the control of disciplines of consenting and authorizing community. They serve God's purposes of preserving the fallen creation in the course of the history of reconciliation, or they do not serve it at all. One cannot explain that history or enter it without attending fully to the expectations of following Jesus, but the history itself is the theological context for understanding war.

Much more formidable arguments in favor of pacifism, that is, rejection of violence, are those put forth by Stanley Hauerwas and John Howard Yoder. What makes them so substantial is that they are grounded in essential theological foundations, in the nature and ways of God, and not in the first instance in a principled rejection of violence. Hauerwas writes that "pacifism is not first of all a prohibition, but an affirmation that God wills to rule his creation not through violence and coercion but by love. . . . Pacifism is the form of life that is inherent in the shape of Christian convictions about God and his relation to us."[5] The first point here pertains to how God rules his creation, namely, by love. That is true in the ultimate sense, in that the love of God wills a new creation through renewal and reconciliation. In the instrumental sense, however, the Bible makes clear that God rules also through divine wrath, reproach, and judgment, and through particular

---

5. Hauerwas, "Pacifism: Some Philosophical Considerations," 99.

nations as the "rod of the Lord" chastising the people of God. Any of these may be ways of expressing divine love, but they are not inherently nonviolent. The second point has to do with the shape of the Christian life. To that one must reply that it is shaped by the vocation to enter and engage God's work of reconciling the fallen creation. As I shall show in what follows, the process of reconciliation presupposes God's preservation of what has rebelled against God. Preservation involves uses of power, and power includes an element of coercion.

In *The Politics of Jesus*, John Yoder wrote,

> If what we have said about the honor due the Lamb makes any sense, then what is usually called "Christian pacifism" is most adequately understood not on the level of means alone, as if the pacifist were making the claim that he can achieve what war promises to achieve, but do it just as well or even better without violence. This is one kind of pacifism, which in some contexts may be clearly able to prove its point, but not necessarily always. That Christian pacifism which has a theological basis in the character of God and the work of Jesus Christ is one in which the calculating link between our obedience and ultimate efficacy has been broken, since the triumph of God comes through resurrection and not through effective sovereignty or assured survival.[6]

Here Yoder is contrasting a type of pacifism that promises positive results with one that is grounded solely on obedience to the call of God to follow the way of Christ even to the cross. As to the former he says, maybe it will work, maybe not. But the latter is what is meant by Christian pacifism: be obedient to the call, and hope for redemption only through the resurrection. That is a powerful argument. Certainly he is correct in his decision between the two types. The question from my side is whether the call of God essentially is to be obedient to the nonviolent way, or whether it is to enter the divine work of reconciling the fallen creation. If the latter is right, which I believe to be the case, then the requirements of a reconciling ministry define the content of obedience.

War, Sin, and the "Order of Preservation"

Theological thinking about war must involve the whole history of redemptive grace, not one aspect of the story only, and specifically not only or

---

6. Yoder, *Politics of Jesus*, 246.

even primarily sin and its effects. Obviously such thinking must take direct notice of sin, but always in the context of the history of grace, and not as the dimension of human failure that creates its own theological context. That is, the history of redemptive grace including and overcoming sin is the context for theological thinking about war—not the history of sin itself. Nevertheless, the connection between war and sin is so intimate and powerful that it tends to compel theological inquiry to take its departure from the connection, which then also shapes the content of the theology.

The Lutheran tradition divides the forms of divine intervention into three "orders": creation, preservation, redemption. The *order of preservation* is the context for thinking theologically about war, because preservation is the divine intention and mode of intervention to protect what God has created against the worst consequences of the fall into sin. This activity of divine presence is manifest institutionally in the state, which serves the cause of preservation by turning the effects and energies of sin against themselves, for the purpose of maintaining order at home and defending people and territory against attacks from outside. In the latter case it conducts war, and does so, when justified, as an instrument of preservation against the effects of sin.[7]

There are important affirmations in this view, in addition to its commitment to give serious and fundamental attention to the reality of sin. One is that state and war are not present in the original divine plan, and therefore are not elements in the order of creation. The other is that the state is not a redemptive institution, has no presence in the fullness of the kingdom of God, and therefore is not of the order of redemption. The state and its instrument of war serve the order of redemption by maintaining the fallen creation in existence, and by holding it open for the proclamation of the Gospel.

I agree with these theological affirmations, but I do not see that they make the case for concentrating theological inquiry into war in the so-called order of preservation. The state as an institution of the fall is not present in original creation; nevertheless, there is an ordering of power in the original plan of God that is not simply replaced by the state. The organic elements of power both come to expression in the state and seek to give it normative direction. The state, as I have said, is not itself a redemptive institution; it must not be allowed to usurp the role and functions of the church.

---

7. For a recent and very prominent Lutheran interpretation of the state and war, see Thielicke, *Theological Ethics*, vol. 2, *Politics*.

But the redemptive activity of God embraces even the state and war, and strives by grace to discipline the violence of the former to the consent and authority of developing community, and to move the latter toward more complete achievements of the prospects for peace. This redemptive activity is manifest most completely in the history of grace, which therefore is the necessary starting point for theological thinking about war.

The Just War (or Justified War) Ethic

The just war ethic is another frequent starting point for Christian thinking about war.[8] The case for it usually is that states will in fact fight wars, and in light of that inexorable tendency the morally responsible—and indeed the theologically responsible—effort should be to limit the occasions for resort to war and also the damage done in wars when they do occur. This ethic essentially is about justification for the use of force. It has developed historically into the two critical categories of *ius ad bellum* (justification for resort to war) and *ius in bello* (moral criteria limiting the actual practice of war).[9] This alternative to pacifism is of great importance, at least for those who do not reject all war on principle yet do not agree that in war everything is permissible.

The problem with this ethic for specifically Christian thinking is that it does not have an explicit theological foundation, even though it has theological elements and—as some see it—may be anchored in love of God and neighbor.[10] In fact, its provisions and criteria can be separated from theology and made into a secular ethic with no theological framework, guidance, or limitation.[11] The absence of an explicit Christian theological framework, with the possibility of its being separated out into a purely secular ethic, exclude a possible role as the principal guide for Christian

---

8. For an authoritative study of historic Christian views on war, see Bainton, *Christian Attitudes toward War and Peace*.

9. Paul Ramsey was the principal Protestant contributor to just war theoretical development and analysis in the second half of the twentieth century. See especially his *War and the Christian Conscience*; *The Just War*; and *Speak Up for Just War or Pacifism*. For a more recent analysis, see O'Donovan, *The Just War Revisited*. My own early contribution is *Modern War and the Pursuit of Peace*.

10. See Bell, *Just War as Christian Discipleship*.

11. A forthright and commendable example of this—nontheological—case for the justified war ethic is Atack, *The Ethics of Peace and War*.

war-thinking—even if it does in fact have some usefulness for clarifying issues of justification for the uses of military force.

When the justified war ethic is incorporated into God's work of reconciliation, the theology transforms some of its basic aspects. I shall explore this claim in a later chapter. Here I suggest two points: 1) the context of the history of grace rearranges the importance of the criteria of resort to war and assigns priority to the criterion of just intention, not to just cause, inasmuch as the primary content of just intention ought always to be the restoration or creation of peace between the belligerents, whatever the cause of conflict may be; 2) the same context of the history of grace stretches out the time and space in which issues of justice and justification are to be determined. This "stretching out" allows and encourages reflection on how all parties have contributed to the creation of the problem, and in doing so invites—and indeed requires—confession, repentance, and forgiveness. It recognizes moral responsibility and moral analysis as permanent elements of the exercises of power, and does not limit the role of moral inquiry to a point in time when the "moral issue" arises.

I must emphasize that this book is not another study of the just war tradition and the ethic arising from it. I have written on that topic in the past, and I encourage further inquiry into the just war ethic's reasoning, applications, and theological sources. The issue here is to discern and explore the wider theological context of that ethic and in doing so to provide a framework for its review and reconsideration.

Invitation to a Conversation in Faith

Both modes of inquiry—the theological and the political—are fundamental to the project; nevertheless, I privilege the theological aspect, because I am writing as a churchman—a pastor, preacher, theologian, and theological educator—and not as a would-be policymaker or pundit. I write for the purpose of inviting members of the community of faith into an ongoing and vital conversation. When I engage in extended explorations into political meanings, I do so in order to show what is involved in the political incarnation of the doctrine of reconciliation, not to score points with or provoke specialists in the fields of foreign policy and political theory. I want to encourage people of the church to explore the relationship more fully and faithfully, to think more profoundly and critically about the meaning of reconciliation, and in doing so to equip themselves better to engage in faith the threats, the crises, and the challenges of war. Persons who are interested in the policies and practices of war, but who are not inclined to pursue theological inquiry, may find something useful here. If so, that is a welcome result, but an incidental one. I intend the book to be an offering to those who are or aspire to be "stewards of the mysteries of Christ," but who understand also that as stewards they must deal with the uglier aspects of human existence. Nevertheless, if it is true, as I maintain, that war is inherently a theological problem, it will be impossible to arrive at a full understanding of its reality by nontheological methods alone. That is another reason for privileging a theological inquiry.

For those who want to compare theological and nontheological methods for understanding the relation of reconciliation and war, I recommend William J. Long and Peter Brecke's *War and Reconciliation: Reason and Emotion in Conflict Resolution*.[12] It is a very good book with a title similar to this one. It is not at all theological but is well worth reading for its historical and social scientific studies of reconciliation processes in domestic and international conflicts. By comparing the two, one can see the differences in method between a book that is both theological and political, and one that is strictly political.

Those who are looking for analyses of and policy proposals for particular hot spots in international relations will not find them here. As I have indicated, this book is a methodological exercise in *how to think* as Christians. The method can be adapted to other types of problems. It is not focused on case studies, nor are its implications for war only.

Doubtless some critics of this work will maintain that the approach is a very American one, that the discussions of power betray the national location of the author. I do not dispute the point. Everyone who makes an inquiry into war and peace shaped by the central doctrines of the Christian faith must construe the issues from his or her own location in time and space. So it is with me and my own efforts. I cannot purport to rise above the strenuous and at times appalling challenges of my own country's vast power and its disposition and contend for a one-size-fits-all Christian formula. The point, however, is to offer the invitation to thinking about the problems from the standpoint of faith, which also means concretely from whatever place in human society the Almighty has chosen to settle us.

---

12. Long and Brecke, *War and Reconciliation*.

How I Got Here

In 1958 Emory University hired me as a newly minted PhD to teach what they called "Religion and the Political Order" in the Candler School of Theology and the newly organized Graduate Division of Religion.[13] Through the succeeding decades I developed and taught courses dealing with ethics and international politics, Christian political thought, peace and war, the churches and international conflict, and Reinhold Niebuhr, in addition to the broader courses in Christian ethics and a denominationally specific course on John Wesley's ethics. From the beginning I insisted on grounding my teaching and writing theologically, and early on I became convinced that the doctrine of reconciliation was that true and necessary grounding. I saw it as the defining representation of the work of God in Christ, and therefore the framework for all Christian thinking and vocation. I directed this focus pedagogically into a course titled "The Theology and Ethics of Reconciliation," in which I encouraged students to develop a coherent and biblically grounded theology to guide and permeate all of their pastoral work, and especially to shape and inform their preaching. The two sets of concerns—theological and political—issued also in a number of published essays on reconciliation and various aspects of life, especially international politics.[14] My presidential address (1989) to the Society of Christian Ethics in the United States and Canada applied the theology of reconciliation to the theme of "Truth and Political Leadership."[15]

The present essay carries these issues forward by exploring the relationships among war, peace, and reconciliation. Given the nature of my background and interests, one would expect it to be both theological and political. Given the nature of the topic, it cannot be one without the other.

A Note on War

For purposes of this inquiry I am limiting the meaning of war primarily to armed conflict between or among states. The focus of reconciliation and peace in this case is on war as a social institution inhabiting the web of relationships among more or less discrete entities that like to represent themselves as sovereign states. In doing so, I am excluding the metaphorical

---

13. Now renamed, appropriately, the James T. Laney School of Graduate Studies.
14. *Modern War and the Pursuit of Peace.* See further entries in the bibliography.
15. *Annual of the Society of Christian Ethics* (1989), 3–19.

applications of the term *war*, such as "war on drugs," "war on terrorism," "war on crime," and the like. The massive concentrations of efforts in such cases often reach across state lines, but they do not inherently involve conflict among the states. If they do so, then they become occasions of interstate war. Also, I mean to set aside reference to revolutionary movements with no direct and immediate relevance to the state system, although the development of the argument may have implications for these movements as well.[16] That is especially so when states must use their military capabilities to oppose sub- or nonstatal mobilizations of force that aim to destroy existing states or to enter into the interstate system by seizing control of particular states.

In theoretical terms, war is a negation of the web of relationships that constitutes the international system, substituting for the relationships various degrees and kinds of violence as means of resolution, communication, and peacemaking. It is also the unraveling of the civilizing process, inasmuch as it weakens or eliminates rules governing and restraining international behavior. This theoretical definition allows us to acknowledge changes in warfare across the years and to move ahead with the issues of politics and reconciliation. War changes, of course, and continues to do so. It involves whole nations and not armies only, and increasingly the prospect of cyberwarfare. It is reshaped by communications and technology. The emergence of nuclear weaponry and delivery systems not only extends the destructive and deterrent power of states but also generates its own characteristic technological-political system. Asymmetrical warfare allows stateless forces to attack powerful states at their points of weakness. The historically European theater of war becomes global. War indeed may become intercivilizational—a "clash of civilizations"—and not only interstatal.[17] None of these changes in warfare moves the phenomenon outside the connectedness of the international system, nor converts it from a conflict involving states to something entirely different.

16. Long and Brecke, *War and Reconciliation*, study both international and domestic conflicts and conclude that the prospects for reconciliation are much stronger for the latter than the former, with some exceptions. They write, ". . . the role of reconciliation events as a means for conflict resolution is substantially different between nations than it is within nations. Factors associated with forgiveness that act to restore order in civil conflict cases are largely absent in international cases. Yet, unlike the civil conflict cases, negotiated bargains *can* work to restore order between nations when reconciliation events constitute effective signals of a desire for improved relations by their costly, novel, voluntary, and irrevocable nature."

17. Huntington, *The Clash of Civilizations*.

Of course, one may argue that the state itself is phasing out of existence, challenged by forces that are economic in one dimension and civilizational in another. Yet however prominent and influential these forces become, they do not eliminate the power and centrality of the states. I shall deal with this question later. Here I point out that the states are the primary controllers of the weaponry and other means of warfare. When war breaks out, including asymmetrical war, the primary aim of opponents is to diminish or capture the war-making capabilities of states. The continuing reality of war is as a social institution in the international system, of which the fundamental component is the state system.

If the nation-state is not yet destined for extinction, neither—sadly—is interstate war. As I write, Israel is contemplating whether it should destroy Iran's incipient nuclear weapons capability before Iran can use a developed capability to destroy Israel. Venezuela, Colombia, and Ecuador are augmenting their military establishments to deal with reciprocal threats, real or imagined. India and Pakistan—both nuclear powers—muscle each other over Kashmir instead of focusing on the more real and immediate threats from domestic terrorist groups. China bullies other states in its region to enforce territorial claims and expands its "blue water" navy. Syria seems to be imploding as a state, and its internal conflict has invited interstate antagonisms into its civil strife. Russia is using its armed forces to bully the Ukraine, while risking wider military conflict. North Korea, well . . .

Most of Europe has learned how to overcome its long history of militant hostility and military disasters, but much of the world has not yet found the way to create this "paradise"—to use Robert Kagan's term.[18] And some observers worry that Europe's "paradise" may not survive major and extended economic crises. Regrettably, there are still reasons to address the problems of war and peace in the interstate system. To do so in the context of reconciliation remains as a necessity of Christian faith.

To Continue . . .

With this sketch of the project set forth, we move on to examine the theological and political contexts of war and their interaction. The interaction is fraught with numerous conflicts and contradictions between reconciliation and war, none so profound and momentous as the radical contrast between the inherent natures of the two terms. To that problem we must turn first.

18. Kagan, *Of Paradise and Power*.

2
War and Reconciliation: Logics and Contexts

Exploring the relationship of reconciliation to war is a daunting task, because the inner logic of reconciliation and the inner logic of war stand in sharp opposition to each other. Reconciliation moves toward the reunion of the separated—Paul Tillich's definition of love—on terms that embody justice, respect, and genuine authority in the using of power. Its logic is the way of empathy, repentance, forgiveness, mutual recognition of particular interests and the search for common interests—a quest for community that transforms belligerents into members who depend on the fabric of community and on each other. War, by contrast, moves toward the total defeat of one party by the other, the unilateral imposition of terms of settlement, the authority of victorious power derived from superiority of force, the willful destruction of whatever stands in the way of these outcomes. Its logic, in Clausewitz's description, is the unrelenting, unlimited use of violence to achieve the defeat of the enemy—a teleology unrestrained by moral or psychological limits. Including the term *peace* as a link between war and reconciliation does not resolve the opposition. Peace is a particular organization of power, an outcome of the struggle, not a commanding ideal imposed from without. It too is compromised and often controlled by the conflict of logics.

How, then, is it possible to think about war in the light of Christian faith when the two governing modes of thinking, that is, the logics of reconciliation and war, are contradictory? These ways of thinking simply run on separate tracks, requiring forms of action that intersect as train wrecks but not coming together to cooperate or transform. The reality of contradictory logics implies that war will proceed on its destructive way, treating appeals to reconciliation only as annoying and confusing divergences, or as signs of weakness inviting aggression. That reality tends to consign reconciliation to the realm of personal relations and idealistic dreams, with no concrete prospects for using power in the interest of justice or fashioning more integral community beyond the enmities of conflict. The ways of war and the ways of faith appear to be alternate constructions of reality that cannot be thought together.

It is possible to think them together. The two logics, so-called, are not independent elements running their own discourses and controlling their own operations. They exist in contexts, to which they give direction and meaning but which also subject them to contextual limits. That is clear, certainly, in the case of war. In his *Pentagon's New Map*, Thomas P. M. Barnett criticizes the Pentagon for thinking of war only in the context of war instead of in the context of everything else.[1] His reasoning behind the distinction is that resort to military force does not disconnect from the rest of social reality when war breaks out and the military instruments of foreign policy seem to displace the other instruments. Although war is a social institution with its own rules and notions of value, it is also an institution of a particular historical order and must be understood and prosecuted in relation to other elements of that order. Barnett's contention is that the primary element in the *everything else* is globalization, and that whatever pertains to war—including its avoidance, its threat value, and its direct use in support of foreign policy objectives—must be governed by the realities and implications of globalizing tendencies. Globalization therefore becomes the principal and essential nonmilitary context for interpreting and planning the role of war. It is also the historical process in which war is assigned any rationality it possibly may have.

I agree with Barnett in his insistence on attending to the larger context of war, and I am informed—somewhat cautiously—by his particular focus on globalization. But I want to look more specifically than he does at the context of politics—that aspect of *everything else* most proximate to war and most responsible for its rationale and prosecution. Also, I want to investigate in considerable detail the context of reconciliation, fundamentally in its theological character—something that does not come into view at all in Barnett's understanding of the *everything else*. Later I shall give some attention to his argument concerning globalization. For the present, let us note that these questions of context have both theoretical and historical

---

1. Barnett, *The Pentagon's New Map*.

dimensions. In actual practice, they are dimensions of the same reality. Hence one can inquire into the theoretical dimensions of context while understanding also that they are inquiries into the particularities of history.

The identification of the contexts of war and reconciliation, and of the role of the logics therein, will give us clues as to how faithful thinking about war might be possible. Let us begin our inquiry into the contexts of the logics by considering the political-historical context of war.

The Logic of War in Political Context

The triumph of the historical reality of war over the logic of war was clear to Carl von Clausewitz, the Prussian officer and military theorist to whom I referred earlier. I set up the conflict between the logics of reconciliation and war originally by citing his claim that war is the unrelenting and unlimited use of violence to achieve total defeat of the enemy. That is true, in his estimation, but only if war is considered a phenomenon in and of itself and without reference to some important qualifications that he sets forth concerning war's logic. For one thing, he makes a distinction between "absolute (theoretical) and real war."[2] The theory of war is expressed in the logic of absolute violence. The reality of war is found in the concreteness of its practice, when various factors in the historical situation intervene to limit the force of the logic. He refers to these factors as the "nonconducting medium" that limits the voltage delivered by the shock of absolute logic. "That nonconducting medium is composed of the great number of interests, forces and circumstances in the existence of the state which are affected by the war."[3] Simply put, the logic of war drives the use of the military instrument, but it is deflected and at times overwhelmed by the historical reality of war. Interpreters of Clausewitz often see only his delineation of the logic of war, and do not notice his recognition of war's historicity.[4]

2. Clausewitz, *War, Politics, and Power.*

3. Ibid., 201.

4. For example, Jean Bethke Elshtain appears to depoliticize Clausewitz, interpreting him in terms of his abstract analysis of the logic of war, and not recognizing how he draws war into the context of politics. She writes that for him "war is an activity that knows no necessity save the rule of force." Also, "Clausewitz is the architectonic champion of, in his words, the theory of 'war itself.' War has an ideal form and to be understood properly must be grasped as a 'pure concept'—unburdened . . . by caveats and modifications" (*Sovereignty*, 151–52). That is true if one is looking only at Clausewitz's analysis of war as "pure concept," but if that alone is true of him, how does one explain

A second qualification set by Clausewitz, and the one that is central to the whole range of his thinking, is his locating of the logic of war in the authenticating and limiting context of politics. In practice war does not run simply according to its own internal logic but serves the political purposes of which it is an instrument. These purposes impose significant limits on both the strategy and tactics of war. Moreover, the state's employment of the instrument of war—along with other instruments of state power—is an aspect of continuing interaction with other states, both allies and opponents—another dimension of encompassing political reality. More about that in a later chapter. One must acknowledge here that if the political purposes are narrowed to total destruction or domination of the opponent, and if the factors in the "nonconducting medium" are not sufficiently resistant, the historical gap between absolute (theoretical) and real war can constrict almost to the point of disappearance. In such cases the logic of war would dominate this history, in large part because of the fashioning of political objectives. In other cases, the influence of the logic might be greatly subdued.

All of this is to say that the so-called logic of war is not war's sole determining factor, and it is not self-enforcing. War must be understood and engaged in the context of politics, broadly and comprehensively understood. This political contextualization, always historically configured, changes the conditions of the conversation between war and reconciliation. The conversation is not between reconciliation and war in a direct sense, but between reconciliation and the political structures and processes in which war has its reason for being and its justifications and limitations.

The Logic of Reconciliation in the Context of Grace

The logic of reconciliation also must be understood from within an encompassing context, but in this case the context is itself reconciliation—theologically defined. The context is the history of God's activity in recovering and developing the wholeness of the fallen creation. It is a history of reconciliation, revealed in its fullness in God's presence in Jesus Christ. The reconciling work of God, which comes to fulfillment in Jesus Christ, is the context of the existence of the created order from its beginning through all its historical transitions. All of the fallen creation, all politics, all war, all globalization, all efforts to overcome creation's brokenness exist within the

---

"War is an instrument of *Politik* carried on by other means"? The political context of war imposes many caveats and modifications.

redeeming grace of God. The logic of reconciliation is, on the one hand, the Spirit of God driving the efforts toward recovery and wholeness, and on the other hand, the delineation of qualities that human beings must bring to expression as they cooperate with the divine work. It is the logic of grace moving through everything that happens from creation through the fall into sin to the final consummation of God's work. It is also the disclosed definition of life in community under the reign of God.

As I have indicated, politics and war exist within this context of divine gracious activity, not outside of it. War and reconciliation exist historically in extraordinary tension with each other, but they are not remote and exclusive entities. War is contextualized in politics, and reconciliation is incarnate—however uncomfortably—in political existence. The examination of the relationship of war and reconciliation proceeds from that point, not from the absolute exclusiveness of the two logics.

As we have seen from our examination of Clausewitz's views, the context of politics blunts the force of the logic of war, constraining it from developing historically in the direction of its theoretical absoluteness. Must the same be said of the logic of reconciliation in the context of divine reconciliation? Is there something about the "pure logic" of reconciliation that makes it inherently unable to engage political reality, and especially the elements of war—without diminishing the force and the quality of the logic? The answer is yes, if one means by reconciliation a method and conclusion grounded exclusively in self-giving love, employing only nonviolent means, and renouncing any contact with or reliance on power. Such conditions point reconciliation to the purity of absolute pacifism, but not necessarily to the overcoming of strife in a reconciled community. The answer is no if the Christian meaning of reconciliation points away from the primacy of methods and attitudes to participating in the reconciling work of God. In that event one must do whatever God does to pursue the renewal of the fallen creation. That implies, among other things, sharing in the work of preservation, which involves engaging in the employment and reorganization of power to promote a higher level of peace.

The context of reconciliation implies and requires direct engagement with politics, war, and violence, and therefore does not support an absolutist, nonhistorical, nonpolitical understanding of reconciliation itself. Reconciliation, theologically defined, is not an abstract ideal that hangs above conflict. It is a direct engagement with whatever is to be found within the context, and therefore with the conflictual elements themselves. But that is not to say, correctly, that the context "blunts the force" of the logic, and reduces it to something that does not actually do the reconciling work. Rather, one should say that the logic of reconciliation repudiates a purely "spiritual" relationship, and acts as a force incarnate in the historical reality of politics of war. It is a transforming influence; in order to transform it must engage power and institutions while at the same time attempting to reset the terms on which they operate and the goals that they pursue.

It follows that the logic of reconciliation is not a method distinct from politics with its power components of consent and force. It is a commitment to encounter force while both limiting its application and effects, and reducing its prominence by enhancing consent and the creation of community. Obviously, therefore, it is not to be equated with pure pacifism or with nonresistance or nonviolent direct action (even though it may make extensive situational use of the latter). Reconciliation as logic is a guide for dealing with problems of politics and war within the context of divine reconciliation. It is not a simple and superior alternative to making decisions with politically powerless means.

Contradictory Logics in Historical Experience

One can see from these analyses that the logics of war and reconciliation are located in each case in a clarifying and authenticating context, and that each is embedded in history. When the contexts are brought into view and explained, the contradictions are less stark and inexorable, even though they are not removed altogether. Nor will they be removed altogether; fundamental tensions remain. Nevertheless, conversation becomes possible, and therefore one can begin to explore the relationship between reconciliation and war in given historical settings.

The further thing to bear in mind is that in actual experience we are talking about history, not logic. In the course of actual conflict often there are occasions when opposing sides do in fact reconcile, at least in the sense of stopping the killing and working out some kind of arrangement with which they can live—for a while, in any event. Whether one should consider these arrangements to be reconciliation in any permanent sense, or certainly in any theological sense, is an issue we must pursue later. For the present let us record that in history the pertinent conflicts involve persons and groups, not abstract and independent logics. If there is any engagement between reconciliation and war, any "conversation," so to speak, it is not between two logics. It is a process of reflection in the consciousness of persons who refuse to reduce the realities of war to the simplest dimensions of empirical experience, or to limit the role of reconciliation to individual relationships or "spiritual" matters. Conversation as reflection moves toward the achievement of a will to discuss rather than simply to fight, toward the recognition of limits to the imposition of force, toward the discovery of common values and the formulation of a language of political discourse, and toward the institutionalization of these elements of sociality, giving them stability and continuity. Thus there are possibilities in the realities of history, if not in the abstractions of logic, for investigating the interactions of reconciliation and war.

The Method: Analyzing the Contexts

What we have learned thus far is that the juxtaposition of logics is not the way to establish the engagement of reconciliation with war. Each of the logics is clarified when viewed in its pertinent and appropriate context. Politics is the context for understanding the reality of war as actually experienced. The history of divine grace, which is the account of God's maintenance and recovery of the fallen creation, is the context for understanding reconciliation. The method of engaging reconciliation and war therefore is a process of analyzing the two contexts in order to discover how the analysis discloses the possibilities of conversation and resultant action. In doing so, however, we must recognize that the two contexts are not separate worlds but different ways of viewing and experiencing the same reality. In fact, if war exists in the context of politics, politics and war exist in the context of the history of divine grace. Each contextual analysis contributes to the understanding of the other context, but the inclusive context—the fundamentally revealing one—is the history of divine reconciling grace.

We shall proceed by examining the two contexts at length—first the theological, and then the political. The reason for establishing this order is the one given: the history of divine grace is the comprehensive context and the one that discloses the ultimate reality of both politics and war. With that part of the process behind us, we shall be ready to reflect theologically on the political processes and relationships, inquiring into the method of reconciliation itself as disposition and means for engaging the problem of war.

Some Matters of Necessity

Earlier I raised the question whether conversation between the two logics is possible. Before leaving this discussion I must insist that the effort to bring reconciliation and war into some kind of constructive engagement is necessary. The necessity is on both sides. Reconciliation is the conclusive definition of the work of God and the determining form of the Christian life. War, with its destructive rage, is the ultimate challenge for both. To renounce the possibility of conversation is to admit defeat both for the divine effort to recover and renew the fallen creation and for the vocation of Christians to participate faithfully in that work. That is one side. The other is that by waving off any possible interaction with reconciliation war would be surrendered to its own internal and destructive dynamics. Studying war in the context not only of politics but also and especially in the history of divine redeeming grace is the way to discern both the fundamental reality of which war is the disruption and the terms for overcoming its disruptive consequences.

PART ONE
The Theological Context

3

The History of Divine Grace: The Context of Reconciliation

Reconciliation as Divine-Human History

A theological approach to the problem of war should begin with inquiry into God and the nature and ways of God. The temptation, however, is to begin with an empirical and historical reading of war and ask what God has to do with it. Only then, supposedly, do we get some clues as to what God is doing in the world, or in this case, in the world at war.[1] Yet if one is going to ask questions about what God is doing in the world, one should begin with God and not with the world—or at least with an inquiry into how God

---

1. A generation ago liberation theologians, especially those with Latin American commitments, looked for guidance for Christian theology and action from the question, what is God doing in the world? Their notable answer: God is tearing down unjust structures and building new ones, new structures that are truly just and not compromised by the oppression built into existing institutions and power arrangements. "Tearing down and building up" is a characterization of divine worldly activity arrived at by first making social scientific analyses of the situation of conflict and then thinking theologically about it. I never was convinced the proponents of this method actually were using it in that order of procedure, because it was clear to me that they took a theological stance at the outset in support of the societal victims and then made their social scientific analyses before going on to more analytical and constructive theological efforts. I shared their moral commitments but questioned the rightness of their theological method, and therefore to some extent the rightness of their theological results. Had they begun their approach with an understanding of God as reconciler, they would not have surrendered their commitment to justice, but would have been less gnostic in their quest for liberation from historic structures and more inclined to ask how to fashion self-limiting structures that would control their own future exercise of power.

relates to the world. There is, of course, no straight theological line running from God to war—nothing self-evident, so that when one says "God" one in consequence understands "war." How then should we proceed with our inquiry?

We do that by examining the history of God's relationship to the world, that is, to what God has created, and to what has happened to that creation in its own history. The quest in this examination is not about events in human time, discerned through established methods of historical study, but about the inner meaning of the biblical story, the connecting and revelatory narrative, discerned by faith. It is engagement with the Bible in its wholeness, and not as a disparate collection of canonical texts. The Bible as a whole is about the history of God's relationship to what God has created and to what humankind has made of it. It is a history of divine grace, its intentions and its workings, a history of sin, rebellion, and recovery. It is also the context in which one must study politics and war in order to learn what is missing from nontheological accounts, and to discern the terms of conversation between war and faith.

When we spell out the history schematically, in classical form, we say that God created out of nothing, that humankind spoiled and distorted the creation through sin, that God brought it under judgment yet preserved it against its violent and fragmenting tendencies, and that God acted in Christ to begin the process of making it whole again. These are the majestic themes of creation, fall, judgment, preservation, and salvation. They are what the Bible and its supporting and generating faiths are all about. Without the substance and unifying power of this history, the particular texts and passages do not add up to a clear, consistent, and redeeming message. In the light of this history, we can discern the meaning and relevance of seemingly discordant and disparate texts and passages, and we arrive—inevitably and inexorably—at the divine work of reconciliation.

The history is the totality of God's relationship to what God has created. The key to this history is what appears at the end of the list of modes of relationship: God in Christ reconciling the world to the divine self, and therefore to its own original purpose and possibilities. When I say that reconciliation is the key to the history, I mean it is the interpretive principle of that history, not simply its end-term. It is the clue to its meaning. That is, we must not think of the history of God in relation to the fallen creation only in terms of stages of that history, as though it led up to a climax set apart from what went before. Rather, once we grasp the meaning of the end-term, we must look back across the whole of the history from that point to understand what God has been doing throughout and why God has been doing it. From the occasion of the fall, God has been engaged in redemptive work, judging the failures and rebellions, preserving the world in order to save it, reopening the meaning of creation in order that its divinely given possibilities may be realized. That is the biblical story in its fullness. It is a history of redemption—of healing, renewal, recovery. The themes are blended throughout; they do not characterize distinct phases or dispensations. God's work of reconciliation ties them all together and illuminates them.

Reconciliation in the Pauline Text

Having claimed that the whole character of this history is a history of divine reconciliation of the fallen creation, one must turn to the Bible to ask about the fuller meaning of the term itself and therefore of the historical narrative. What does reconciliation mean in the biblical record? To be perfectly honest, there is not much in the Bible as a whole that deals specifically with reconciliation—which, after all, is the representation of divine activity under reference here. Much of the Old Testament, or Hebrew Bible, is concerned not with reconciliation among peoples but with the victory of God the Warrior over the enemies of God's chosen people.[2] Explicit statements in the New Testament are few, and mainly they come not from the Gospels but from letters of Paul or literature in the Pauline tradition.

Several of these passages have been of enormous historical importance in establishing the meaning and reality of reconciliation in the heart of the Christian message. One text in particular stands out as the foundation of Christian teaching on the subject. It is Paul's famous declaration in 2 Cor 5:18–19: "All this is from God, who reconciled us to himself through Christ, and has given us the ministry of reconciliation; that is, in Christ God was reconciling the world to himself, not counting their trespasses against them, and entrusting the message of reconciliation to us" (NRSV).

This Pauline text tells us, first of all, that the work of God is reconciliation—"reconciling the world to himself." Reconciling is what God does. It is what God does in Christ, and as such it is a rendering of divine work and presence far transcending the concern in the Synoptic Gospels to re-establish the kingdom of God in Palestine by expelling the Romans.

2. See, for example, von Rad, *Holy War in Ancient Israel*.

Furthermore, the object of divine reconciliation is the world, the *kosmos*, which in this case means the whole of the fallen creation. The reconciling work of God is inclusive—totally. Reconciliation is what God does throughout the universe, across the past, through the present, and into the future. It includes the rescue and restoration of individuals, of human society, and of nonhuman nature. It is neither an individualistic concept nor an anthropocentric concept. That is, it is not focused only on how individual persons get along with each other, and it is not preoccupied so completely with the human elements of the creation. Everything in God's creation is included in God's reconciling work in Christ. Obviously, politics and war exist within and not outside of the context of reconciliation—along with everything else. God's reconciling work in Christ contextualizes God's relationship to the (fallen) creation.

Reconciling to *himself*—that is a large subject requiring quite a bit of exploration, most of it not here. Basically, it is a matter of bringing the fallen creation to recover and develop the intentions God has for it, especially by recovering the defining relationship to God. In human reference, it refers fundamentally to recovery of the whole image of God, and therefore to the overcoming of all the negatives introduced and perpetuated by human sin—opposition, animosity, hatred, egoism, corruption, disruption, strife—everything that represents the brokenness and distortion of the original creation. By implication it points to the creation of new community in place of these divisions and defilements. It refers also to the development of what is latent in creation, the mandates implied in placing humankind in a garden to keep and till it, the task of making "the desert blossom as the rose." Development as reconciliation to God is not an Aristotelian notion of rising from potentiality to actuality, but a biblical one of engaging the possibilities of creation as they emerge in history, laden with the distortions of sin, and shaping them decisively for and not against the purposes of God.

The text makes clear that the origins and efficacy of reconciliation are from God, not from human beings. God initiates and continues all the constructive aspects of the relationship. "All this is from God." In formal theological language, it is prevenient grace. God comes before all human action. When human beings enter into the work of reconciling and renewing, they do so in response to the divine action already underway. There is nothing in this passage to support the argument that sinful human beings must seek out and appease an angry God in order to win divine favor. To the contrary, God is the One who initiates the overcoming of animosity, the

One who begins the recovery and renewal. "But God proves his love for us in that while we were still sinners Christ died for us" (Rom 5:8 NRSV). Any engagement with war, seeking to move conflicts toward peace, encounters the reconciling activity of God already at work. There is nothing in the passage to allow the view that war exists outside of the context of divine reconciliation, or that God is absent from war and cannot be encountered there, although certainly it does not minimize the antagonism between divine transforming love and the savagery of human conflict. God initiates and presses the case. God establishes the context. "All this is from God."

Moreover, God's work of reconciliation in Christ is both event and ongoing process. When Paul speaks of "God, who reconciled us to himself through Christ . . ." he is saying that reconciliation is an accomplished fact, not essentially a goal for future striving and achievement. In Rudolf Bultmann's words, ". . . the 'reconciliation' precedes any effort—indeed any knowledge—on man's part, and 'reconciliation' does not mean a subjective process within man but an objective factual situation brought about by God."[3]

The "objective, factual situation" to which Bultmann refers is an event that, once completed, alters the character of the relationship between God, humankind, and all the rest of the *kosmos*. It establishes a new context for everything that exists. On the other hand, Paul writes that "in Christ God was reconciling the world to himself," indicating thereby that the work of reconciliation is both finished and unfinished. It is a process, one that continues on the basis of what has been accomplished already. It is reconciling work in the context of reconciliation. Those who recognize and confess to what God has done already in Jesus Christ are summoned to enter and share in the divine work of reconciliation.

Theologians often have restricted the meaning of reconciliation in this passage to justification, or the forgiveness of sins. They infer that limitation from the words "not counting their trespasses against them." John Wesley, for example, seemed to equate reconciliation with justification, instead of extending it into the whole-making work of God in sanctification.[4] Restricting reconciliation to justification is an error in theological exegesis and practical application. It reduces the scope and extent of God's

---

3. Bultmann, *Theology of the New Testament*, 1:286.

4. See Wesley's "Justification by Faith" (Sermon 5), 181–99. In this sermon Wesley appears to equate reconciliation with justification as the forgiveness of sins and the removal of enmity with God. Neither of these amounts to a full recovery of the image of God, which surely is what reconciliation with God should mean.

reconciling work in Jesus Christ. To grasp the comprehensive meaning of reconciliation, Wesley should have integrated the concept more fully into the order or way of salvation, with its elements of prevenient, justifying, and sanctifying grace. Prevenient grace clearly is intended in the claim that God initiates and continues the transforming process. Justification removes the grounds for enmity between God and humankind. It is the finished, objective work of God. As such, it is essential to reconciliation, but it is by no means the whole of it. Sanctification is the continuation of God's efforts to heal and renew the fallen creation. The entire plan and work of salvation are manifest in God's reconciling work in Christ.

Let us look again, in summary fashion, at the aspects of reconciliation set forth or implied in the Pauline passage. Divine initiative starts the process of recovery. The object of recovery is the entirety of the fallen creation. The objective, completed work of God in Christ resets the relationship. The continuing, reconciling activity of God embraces everything, and also defines and creates the setting for human vocation. The text interprets the history of God's action in relation to the world; the history is the larger framework for the text; the text is itself incorporated into the history. Together history and text reveal the context established by divine action, and therefore the setting for theological inquiry into war and politics.

Delineating and interpreting the history of divine reconciliation makes up for the lack of much explicit biblical attention to the topic. It also provides a larger framework for the Pauline passage, incorporating it into the grand story, providing the means to give it depth and content, and both drawing upon and confirming its christological basis. For our present purposes, the text and the history together establish reconciliation as the theological context for understanding war and politics. War and politics lie within the fallen creation, and therefore in the context of grace that constitutes this history. It is the framework within which they necessarily must be understood. It is a context of judgment, preservation, recovery, renewal, and reconciliation.

Other—Nontheological—Meanings

What God does in the history of God's relationship to the fallen creation *defines* reconciliation. That is the point of my argument thus far. But the term *reconciliation* appears frequently in common usage, including occasions of interstatal conflict when two sides want to quit fighting and move toward some kind of settlement. In those cases their language may sound theological simply because they are speaking reconciliationese, but it is not theological, and it is not biblical. Its sources are different, as are its intentions.

Reconciliation as Deal-Making

Ordinary definitions of the term—including those that appear in the course of stalemated conflict—do not carry the full meaning of *to reconcile*.[5] When folks begin to use the term to refer to a possible next step in an ongoing fight with no apparent victory of one side over the other, usually it is because the belligerents weary of strife—not because they experience a transforming love of their opponents that generates the will to forgive, heal, and renew. The meaning of the term then is drawn from the nature and course of the struggle itself. Reconciliation means, in such cases, that the competing sides will try to strike a deal—one that will allow each side to walk away with something worth saving even if it is less than what they hoped to achieve by fighting. Rarely is the deal accepted as a final resolution. The contestants do not renounce their ultimate objectives with any finality. They do not dissolve their ancient identities and hatreds. They do not see themselves necessarily as joining together in a relationship that opens the way to fashioning a new community in which the old things are put behind them. In fact, they may see this "reconciliation" as a truce during which they rebuild their forces and other assets and plan how to pursue the aims and interests that they never surrendered altogether. If the truce results in the discovery of common interests and the fashioning of new institutions

---

5. In the academic year 1992-93 I was on sabbatical leave at New College, Edinburgh University. In addition to my university affiliation, I served in a minor capacity on the ministerial staff of St. Giles Cathedral, the great church from which John Knox led the Scottish Reformation in the sixteenth century. My first sermon there was titled "The Way of Reconciliation." At that time, the Europeans were exulting over their "reconciliation"—that is, their rejection of war among themselves and their newly found (if not fully developed) ability to cooperate among themselves. In my sermon I pointed out that the New Testament meaning of reconciliation was not the same as the political reconciliation for which they had good reason to rejoice. What they celebrated as reconciliation was combined economic capability to fight the economic threats from the United States and Japan, but especially their freedom from the prospect of war with each other. Those were causes for European celebration, but they were not what I was preaching, nor what the Apostle Paul meant.

to support them, that is all to the good, but it may not be what the erstwhile belligerents had in mind when they decided to reconcile.

Divine reconciliation, by contrast, does not depend for its meaning on the vagaries and tendencies of political conflict. It is not a tentative agreement worked out between or among exhausted belligerents; it is a reality accomplished already in the deed of God, ready to engage the hostilities of human parties with its liberating and transforming power. Its promise to reconcile is a genuine hope for the future, not a truce set up to be violated at an opportune time. "To be reconciled" by the power of God is not to strike a deal. It does not allow for the resumption of conflict when more favorable conditions present themselves. It does not permit the perpetuation of enduring hatreds and ancient, destructive memories resting in the inventory of particular "causes," waiting to be summoned into cohesive action by the newest demagogue on the historical scene. To be reconciled, in biblical terms, is to give honest recognition to the interests of opponents, and to commit to large interests that undergird the needs of all parties—including some needs and interests not included directly in the conflict. It is to seek and offer forgiveness, to publish truth and not propaganda or rationalizations, to initiate common efforts to bind up the wounds of war and to rescue and restore the victims. In a sense that is broad and yet intimate, it means to enter into and continue to create webs of relationship that relativize the ultimacy of the old, particularistic identities that engendered and justified conflict, but without denying and destroying the historic and sociological reality of the enduring identities. These differences from conflict-generated meanings of reconciliation derive from readings of the gracious actions of God. They are not in the first instance discoveries from historical experience or rational inferences from human intentions.

Reconciliation as Return to Earlier Unity

Divine reconciliation also overcomes a fundamental difficulty of using a dictionary definition of reconciliation, namely, "to bind up again." The latter definition presupposes an earlier unity, one expressed perhaps in a common identity and interpreted through common memories. But suppose there is no earlier, broken unity to bind up? The point was made some years ago by the late Dr. Major Jones at an annual meeting of the Society of Christian Ethics in the U.S. and Canada. In a small group discussion focused on racial reconciliation, Dr. Jones, an eminent black ethicist and theologian, commented that he "did not see how we could speak of reconciliation of the races, which implies getting back together again. We never were together." So it is with many other conflicts, including wars between states. "We never were together." How then can we reconcile? How can we "bind up again" that which never was one?

The answer is that the transforming power of divine grace does not require some primal, historical unity to which conflicting parties return. It does not reconcile in that literal sense. It posits a unity existing in the divine creation disordered by human sin. Corporate identities—tribal, racial, religious, ethnic, regional, national—emergent in history entered into that disorder. The grace of God in Christ meets these identities at their point of conflict and invites them into the fashioning of a new creation. It does not require a return to an earlier unity before the disordering took place—that is, to something that never was. It is reconciling in the sense that it recovers for all conflicting parties the image of God, which is definitive of human identity, and opens the possibility of relationships in a new community grounded in this identity. It recovers also the vision of and commitment to the common human vocation, which is the stewardship of all that God has created.

An Etymological Note

Let us note in this regard the etymology of *Versöhnung*, one of the German words for reconciliation. German, a younger language than Latin, was open to Christian theological influence in its formation, whereas Latin—pre-Christian in its formation—was not, at least at this point. The Latin etymology of the term means bringing together again, or binding up again—both of which imply a pre-existing but broken unity. The Latin meaning has no theological significance. This German term for reconciliation is built around the word *Sohn*—son, in English. It is intended generically, of course, as *children*. It refers to the process of becoming children in one family, that is, of becoming children of God. The emphasis is on moving together into a new relationship grounded in divine grace, not on returning to an earlier, historical status of unity. Given the objectivity and efficacy of God's reconciliation, parties to a conflict do not require the memory of an earlier oneness in order to look forward to the transformation of their oppositions and antipathies. Reconciliation means becoming children of God. It is a forward-looking concept remembering a creational unity. Any secular or nontheological use of the term is an analogical application that may not reflect the theological meaning.

Definition and Discernment

The history of grace is the source of knowledge for the right understanding of reconciliation. Any other source is deficient or deceptive. When one looks at the interactions of states and other factors in international politics, the most one sees is the dialectic of integrating and disintegrating.[6] At times one will see evidences of community building and institutional formation in the integrating movements, but they do not define the meaning of reconciliation, nor do they promise it as a confident hope for the future. Always they are accompanied, at least latently, with thrusts toward disintegration, and often will be overwhelmed by them. In theological terms, the possibilities for building community and institutions are manifestations of common grace, and also of the divine work of preservation for humankind in its fallen condition.

The disintegrating tendencies express the persistence of sin manifest in inexorable group egoism, the unrelenting quest for military-based security, and the debasing of human life and identity. The tension in this dialectic, and its pervasive presence throughout human history, make it impossible to use human efforts toward reconciliation as normative definitions, and even less to use them as analogies to explain divine revelation. One must begin with disclosure to faith, and from that source seek to discern the divine intention in war, peace, and reconciliation. One must also use this source to discern the meanings of other elements in the history of grace, and their application to the problem of war.

---

6. For a political scientist's argument for integration-disintegration as the enduring character and future of international society, see Brzezinski, *Power and Principle*.

4

Fundamental Reality and Its Disruptions

War and politics do not *enter* the context of divine grace, nor are they brought into it by human effort—as though their presence there were an avoidable option. No human action is required or even possible to get them there. They exist already in the context of grace, and therefore in the context of divine reconciliation, by reason of the choice and action of God. War is fully understandable—and treatable—only when studied and analyzed in that context. The ultimate reality of war is not defined solely by the conflict of force and interests studied by political scientists. Those conflicts are the foci of attention, of course, but they become fully real and adequately discernible only in the context of the history of God in relation to the fallen creation. When we study war and engage it in that context we gain a clearer grasp of its reality than seen otherwise, and have a more certain—if indeed more daunting—understanding of what to do about it.

What then do we discover when we probe the reality of war in the context of the history of grace, that is, in the story of God's ongoing work to recover and renew—to reconcile—the fallen creation? First of all, we discover that war is a god-making activity—a tendency grounded in the fact that human beings are created for dependence on God, and continue to reach out for God even when they have willed a separation. War expresses that quest, and amplifies it. Also, we discover that war does not escape the fundamental reality of human identity as image of God and corporate human existence as common stewardship of creation, but captures these realities and transforms them with its own disruptive tendencies. And what of the response from the side of God? There is judgment, and there is preservation—all in the context of grace moving toward the reconciliation of the *kosmos* in Christ. And all along the way, of course, there is the question of what kind and quality of transformation can be achieved in human history, and how the answer to that question should affect Christian efforts in dealing with war.

We shall deal with these issues in succeeding chapters, beginning with the defining relationships and realities and their disruption.

War as God-Making Activity

In ordinary reference and experience, war looks like a thoroughly this-worldly phenomenon, to be studied with nontheological methods. Of course, it is that, and the nontheological methods are useful, but fundamentally war is a god-making activity. Unless we discern and grasp that aspect of its nature, we shall not be able to understand why it is so powerful in its control over human life and its ability to command and direct resources needed for other purposes. But why is war a "god-making activity," and what does that imply?

Let us explore these questions by way of the theological psychology and anthropology of St. Augustine, as set forth in his famous prayer: "Thou hast made us for Thyself, and our hearts are restless 'til they find their rest in Thee." According to this view, the fundamental nature of humankind is established in the Creator-creature relationship. Human beings are designed and defined in relation to God. They are truly human and they live in true peace only when they are related rightly and permanently to the One who created them. They love God above all other things, and all other things in relation to God. When they break with that relationship and attempt to live apart from God they fail, because the reality of their God-oriented nature continues with them. They seek for God in everything that they do. They cannot unmake the foundation of their being. As a result they are restless, permanently and unyieldingly restless, in the quest to recover the fundament of their nature without which they cannot be human in the full and proper sense.

In their restlessness, in this drive to find their rest, human creatures fabricate idols and worship them, that is, they will to love and serve particular aspects of created reality as though they were loving and serving God. Thus, the first result of this disruption is that human beings engage perpetually and inexorably in god-making activity. This tendency comes to expression in war, in that war carries the tendency to extremes of group idolization and supports its commitments with violent means. War tends always to transform finite loyalties into ultimate loyalties that have the effect of putting the war-making entity in the place of God, and thereby fabricating a god in the image of their finite loyalties. The passions, commitments, and divisions of war demand an excessively high valuation of and obedience to the nation or other entity making war. In the prosecution of war, particular and relative loyalties and identities are treated as though they are universal and absolute. If war is murderous, which it is, it is also idolatrous. Even when this tendency is restrained by powerful societal conventions, its underlying inclination remains latently active, threatening to destroy the conventions themselves.[1] The result is that war becomes a contest not only between states and military forces but also between or among finite Gods, each of which draws the loyalties and directs the efforts of the contending powers, who fight and kill in the name of their deities.

Of course, that is not a full or sufficient explanation of war, or of why wars occur. Particular wars may be fights over territory, resources, populations, dynastic successions, religious claims, or ideologies. Sometimes they occur because states disintegrate or expand, or because political systems implode or explode. There are wars for aggrandizement, glory, honor, and vengeance (motives rejected by the just war criterion of just intention).[2] However, this absolutizing of particular loyalties is a driving element in war, and it is demonstrable as an empirical tendency. One can discern it without employing a theological methodology. The point, nevertheless, is

---

1. Civilizational solidarity is itself an effective restraint on divinizing and dehumanizing tendencies. That is true, but what also is true is that war helps create the conditions that encourage these tendencies to emerge. The great historian Arnold Toynbee maintained that war is the proximate cause of the destruction of civilization (Toynbee, *War and Civilization*). Military conflict attacks not only the opponent but, by implication and effect, the societal order itself. When prosecuted extensively, it creates social vacuums that invite in demons worse than the ones the use of force sought to expel. Toynbee cited the wars of religion and wars of nationalism as proximate causes—only proximate, in that changes in the societal order induce wars of that type, but "causes" in that they promote and exploit changes in the order that allow and induce the effects described above. Toynbee himself, who wrote often in biblical language, was open to the insight that war, under any conditions, cannot be separated from the restlessness and refocusing that result from human estrangement from God (ibid., 7).

2. Kenneth N. Waltz, in *Man, the State, and War*, discusses various theories of the causes of war, among them the claim that war results from original sin. He disputes single-factor explanations, including that one. He points to the importance of nontheological factors, such as the incompleteness of the international system and the internal problems of particular societies, but allows that sin may be defended as an ingredient element in the origins of conflicts.

that the Augustinian anthropology identifies a tendency inherent in fallen human nature and magnified in war-making, and explains it. Knowing it is there by this means of discernment invites us to look for it and identify it.

Divine Intention and Human Reality

Breaking the relationship with God is the first disruption. There are others that result from this fundamental one. We must consider them, but first we must describe the realities as they exist prior to the disruption, and how they appear as a result of it. These realities are elements of original creation. They are discerned only through disclosure in the history of grace, inasmuch as direct knowledge of original creation is obscured by sin. It is this revealed knowledge that helps us understand more fully the distortions and deceptions of war.

Through the lens of the reconciling history of God we can discern what God intended for humankind and the world in the original design of creation. In this plan humankind exists in relational reality between God and the world. The human creature is image of God. It is not God, because it is a creature, but as creature it images the divine relationship of care and cultivation to the rest of creation. That is the primary meaning of *image of God*: to be like God in exercising the stewarding responsibilities, that is, the care of creation. This image of God is the fundamental reality of human nature. It is the common identity of all human creatures regardless of where they live and how they look and whom or what (if anything) they worship. Genesis chapter 1 declares that the image of God is male and female, and that God gives these human beings dominion over the other creatures. This dominion is for the purposes of care and cultivation, imaging the ways God cares for and cultivates God's creation. Dominion is not for exploitation, nor is it for dividing, conquering, and excluding. Those tendencies appear only when sin enters to spoil the divine plan and corrupt the human beings and their relationships to the rest of creation.

In Genesis 2, the vocational assignment is extended when God places the man in a garden, symbolically the whole earth, and provides him a helpmate, so that together—and equally—they can exercise the caring and cultivating responsibilities God has given them. They are to be stewards of the creation. That is the vocation with which they are endowed by God. The implication throughout is that humankind is a unity. Male and female as God's image are representative of humanity as a whole. Humankind is unified in its nature, its relationship to God, its care for the other aspects of creation. That is the intention of God, obscured in human history as experienced, but revealed in its fullness and authenticity through the reconciling work of God in Christ.

The previous sentence reminds us that in actual experience we do not encounter the human being as divine image, nor do we grasp immediately and unerringly the unity of humankind and the common human vocation to care for the earth. What we encounter are human beings as they have emerged in history, in time and place, not as they appear in original creation. We do not see male and female as image of God; what we see are identities developed naturally in terms of gender and aging and some physical traits, and historically in terms of peoples and cultures and religions. We see hierarchies and priorities, superordination and subordination, preferences and status reflecting worldly values and conditions, but not the divine image. Our experience is that of historical existence, not the pristine clarity of divine creation. That is of great importance, because we may be more aware of differences and particularities than we are of common humanity. Moreover, this historical human existence is sinful existence. Any presence of human beings in history manifests the tendencies of alienation from God and neighbor. These tendencies distort and at times destroy the perceptions of divine image and common human vocation.

Similarly, we do not have impressed upon our senses a common human vocation to care for the earth. More likely, we have a sense of responsibility for smaller parts of the earth and are inclined to get nervous, feisty, and even belligerent when someone else shows too much interest in our particular patch. And others become upset when we show too much interest in their patches. They want to fight to defend them, and feel irresponsible if they do not. On a large scale that means war. Needless to say, that is the opposite of a sense of responsibility given by God to care together for everything created by God. But that is what we experience.

We cannot evade the force of this construction of human existence. There are in fact two realities of human nature, one of them given in creation and disclosed to faith by divine grace, the other known to us in our history and present to experience and investigation. Also, there are two dimensions of worldly responsibility, one to care in common for the whole earth, the other to care as group members for the particular section of the earth to which we seem to be assigned by fate or history or nature. This is duality, but it is not dualistic. They both are real, but they do not split reality into two distinct parts, allowing or requiring us to live fully in one or the other. The two conflicting elements appear together in the same persons and collectivities. Both are true in their representations, and they are not separable. In the light of faith the identity we experience directly and existentially is not unreal by comparison with the image of God, and the uneven, changing, and antagonistic divisions of the world are not in a realm of being separate from the world garden of common human vocation. These empirical facts are who we are in history, in time and place, in relationship to others and to things. The divine design is incarnate in persons and groups visible and spatial and temporal, and in their relationships. There is fundamental human reality (the plan in creation), and there is existential human reality. The former is not a gnostic essence, seeking to break out of the flesh of existence, or an irrelevant and unapproachable ideal; the latter is not an empirical moment with no ontological base and no connection with others of the human species. Both together constitute human reality. We engage in theological and practical error when we attempt to reduce human nature and existence simply to one or the other.

The purpose of viewing human existence through the lens of the reconciling history of God is to discern the intentional, creational reality of human nature not known to us otherwise, and to assert with confidence that it is in fact real to life and practice and without doubt the truth of God. However, even with this means we view it in a glass dimly, because we are discovering its reality in the historical and social substance of beings living in time, not in a so-called state of nature. It is relevant knowledge, both vocationally and in the experience of conflict, because it affords a critical perspective on what actually has happened and is happening, and opens possibilities for changes in direction and practice. We must have in mind this duality of human being when pursuing a theological-critical examination of war and its effects.

As I have said, war is a god-making activity. What are the results when this god-making activity engages the historical realities of human identity and societal commitment that in their original definitions are image of God and the vocation to care for the earth?

Disruption and Its Consequences

War is a contest over space, resources, population, and often of ideas. It comes to full illumination, however, only when one sees it as a disruption of

FUNDAMENTAL REALITY AND ITS DISRUPTIONS

the divine plan for humankind and the world. This disruption is evident in all of the ways set forth above as aspects of God's plan for humanity and the world. Specifically, it changes the fundamental relationship to God, replacing it with idolatrous particular loyalties. It suppresses identity as image of God in favor of identities arising out of social groupings, rejecting common and shared humanity and replacing it with societal commitments that are far less and other than universal. These societal commitments dismiss and displace the common human vocation to care for the earth. Stewardship becomes parochial, armed with violent means to contest the earth with other parochial stewards. That is not what God intends, but that is what war does.

War, in addition to being a god-making activity, also is the occasion and vehicle for changing the identities of all parties to a conflict. It dismisses or displaces the image of God as a representation of human reality and replaces it with purely mundane and particularistic identifications. There is no visibility of the image of God in war, no authority to control action and establish limits. War transforms these historic identities into representations of good and evil, or human and subhuman. It changes the differences of practical diversity, already present in society, to "us versus them." It inflates the self-regard of particular identities, which in turn justifies their sense of superiority, sanctifying the destruction of others as the elimination of lower forms of life and/or as a necessity for protecting humanity as a whole. It invades the normal and natural groupings, transforming them into tribal entities striving for dominance well beyond the needs for simple survival. ("Tribal" is used in this connection to denote any type of grouping—national, racial, religious, etc.—that organizes as in-group, particularizes its identity, and confers ultimate value and meaning on itself and its members over against those who are different and outside.) This "tribal" identity then becomes the locus of human value and the criterion for degrading and destroying any who are not of or in league with the tribe. Image of God as primary human identification no longer plays a role, except where only the members of the tribe are considered truly human and divinely elected. War is dehumanizing, not only of the opponents, but also of those who are members of the tribe. Dehumanizing, in the ultimate sense, means rejecting the limiting and valuing identity as image of God, and replacing it with an identity that is less than and other than the created reality of the human.

Yet another consequence of the disruption is that war displaces or disguises the divine plan for human responsibility in the whole of creation, replacing it with commitments drawn from societal divisions arising naturally out of attempts to reside in and manage the earth. These divisions emerge because people live together in close proximity and depend on each other. There are families, communities, tribes, ultimately nations, and then civilizations. They are less than worldwide simply because the earth is too vast to have a common set of associations. For that reason they also establish divisions of the world's space with responsibilities for care and maintenance that are less than universal. Theologians often speak of these social groups and their divisions of the world's space as aspects of creation itself.

These social groupings, as manifestations of divine creation, are not themselves warlike. Neither sin nor war is present in original creation, but sin is present with the beginning of historical existence, and social groupings as historical formations incorporate the sin that on occasion drives them to war. War presupposes human society with its predictable divisions, and organizes and exacerbates their self-serving inclinations. It engages the human actualities, already manifesting otherness and differentiation, making them competitive and fratricidal and equipping their fratricidal competition with the means and logic of violence. In war the groups confirm the claim to that part of the earth that is their own, and legitimate both its defense and its imperial extension—ideological projections manifesting disruption of the divine intention for tending the garden as humankind's project. War regards the resources of the earth simply as material support for its martial aims and efforts, and in doing so dismisses the divine vocation to care for them in stewardship. In these ways, war disrupts the divine plan. It breaks the oneness of humanity, divides the earth against the intended community of caring, and rejects the common human vocation to care for the creation.

To repeat the fundamental point, these consequences result from the breaking of the defining relationship with God. Their character and their implications emerge into view in the process of discernment informed by the study of war in the context not only of empirical history, but especially in the history of divine grace. The full illumination of the reality of war appears only when war is regarded as a problem of relationship to God, and as the great disrupter of the nature and vocation of humanity created in the divine image. The response of God to this rebellion and disruption involves judgment, preservation, and the limiting and opening of possibilities in history. In every case, however, the response is delivered in the context of redeeming grace.

5

Judgment, Preservation, and Historical Preservation

We have identified and discussed the foundation of the problem: the human disruption of what God has provided and ordained for the welfare of the created order. The displacement of the image of God in favor of other identities and the disruption of the divine plan for common human stewardship of creation generate the line of the history of the fallen creation and continue as commanding characteristics of that history. Put in different words, they create a history of sin and rebellion. What is the divine response, and what are its elements? The overall response is what I have called the history of grace—the efforts of God to heal and renew what human sin has spoiled and set in conflict. Within this history are to be found persistent aspects of divine intervention. Theologians historically have identified them as judgment, preservation, and intra-historical possibilities. We now must examine these elements, each in turn.

But first, let us take note of a fundamental line of inquiry that arises in this examination. It has to do with discernment, or one might say, with revelation. What do we learn about war from looking at it in theological context—something we might not see otherwise? To be technical, we might call this aspect of the inquiry an exercise in theological epistemology—a way of knowing or discovering that gives us a better understanding of how to proceed. First of all, what do we learn about judgment on war, and the related question of divine retribution?

Judgment and War

War brings the fundamental dislocation of the creation-God relationship to violent expression. War is god-making married to political ambition, interest, and ideology—with weapons. It is latent insecurity thrust into visibility and channeled into active drives for expansion and domination. It is the conversion of ordinary human differences to despicable caricatures and justifiable targets. It is killing and destruction in place of diplomacy, dealing, and cooperation. The displacement and disruption produce dreadful and terrifying consequences—experiences of suffering, death, destruction, and despair. And there are other consequences, having to do especially with abandoning stewardship of the whole earth while claiming all or parts of it as national or imperial patrimony, and then fighting over the parochial interests rather than cooperating in the task of tending the garden.

Are these dreadful experiences evidences of the judgment of God? More specifically, are they punishments for the sins of war? Judgment follows upon sin and in response to sin—the original sin that dislodges all creation from its divine moorings, and the particular sins that represent the transgression of God's laws. War is massively sinful in its origins, its mixed intentions, its conduct and its results. Are war and its terrible effects, then, expressions of the wrath of God's judgment?[1]

War, Judgment, and Retribution

The sufferings of war indeed are manifestations of judgment, but they are not divine retribution. They are not punishments for sin. Divine judgment is present, but it is not expressed in wrathful punishments. If judgment were equivalent to punishment, then surely the obvious and severe punishment should fall directly on those whose bad or sinful decisions produced the war, and also on those who conducted it in brutal, illegal, and devastating fashion. In fact, of course, the "guilty" often escape the most punitive consequences, whereas ordinary folks who were not promoting or fighting the war process suffer the greatest devastation and distress. Moreover, the dire effects usually are visited on both or all parties to the conflict, and

---

1. The question at issue is whether the miserable consequences of war should be understood as explicit visitations of God's wrath. It has nothing immediately to do with the matter of appearing before the judgment seat of God to answer for our sins, either at death or at the Great Assize. What that process of judgment means is known only to the mind of God.

especially on their populations, and not uniformly on the side judged to be primarily at fault.

Note in this connection that early on in the development of the just war ethic the rule of conduct in war was to attack only the guilty and avoid harming the innocent. The attack was in support of what was believed to be a just cause, but it served also to punish those accused of provoking the conflict. Subsequently the distinction shifted to attacking combatants while attempting to avoid or minimize damage to noncombatants (the *ius in bello* rule of noncombatant immunity). Why the change? It became evident that the guilty-innocent distinction was not applicable in practice to the complicated and confusing conditions of warfare. Put bluntly, it did not fit the moral distinctions, and therefore made no sense. The soldiers were not necessarily guilty of any wrongdoing, whereas some who were not soldiers might be fully complicit and culpable. Attacks were to be directed against the war-making capabilities of the opponent, avoiding where possible direct and intentional attacks on the civilian population. Doing so would attempt to authorize the justifiable use of military force, while avoiding the insurmountable problem of punishing the guilty in some direct fashion. The point: explaining violence in war as retribution against the guilty is a tough case to make—and perhaps impossible. The killing that takes place in war is not what God intended for humankind, and it may be necessary to serve the just cause for resort to war, but it is not in a direct sense punishment for sin.

But could the wars and their violent actions and effects be God's punishment of the people as a whole for presumed sins that have nothing to do with war as such? Some persons have announced with prophetic certainty that the sufferings of a war are divine visitations for the presence of various forms of sinfulness in the populace, such as swearing, Sabbath-breaking, prostitution, drunkenness, etc. (create your own list).[2] Or could cataclysmic violent events (for example, the attacks of September 11, 2001) be, as some have claimed, divine retribution for alleged national permissiveness with regard to abortion and homosexuality? Whatever one may think of the various practices under reference, the decision to connect them to God's punitive action through the events of war is both defective political analysis and bad theology. It evades serious political and social inquiry into explanations for these acts and events; it presumes to know the mind of God in detail; and it presupposes a concept of collective guilt in assigning

---

2. See, for example, John Wesley's "National Sins and Miseries," Sermon 111 (1775).

blameworthiness to the entire population in its suffering.[3] Making this connection may have more to do with the interests and aims of the advocates of the "punishment" explanation than it does with the realities of war or the intentions of God. There is great suffering in and as a result of war, and there is divine judgment in war, but the former is not an effect of the latter.

But there is such a thing as divine judgment, and it does comes to expression in war. What can such judgment mean, if it is not expressed through punitive retribution? It means that the whole of humankind is under judgment for rejecting the source and foundation of its existence, namely, the love of God above all created things. It has to live in the mess resulting from this rejection. All of humanity, mired in all of the mess. The judgment is that humankind has departed from the only possible way to realize its true humanity, and to realize in their fullness the values of peace, order, and justice. Human existence suffers disorder and disorientation, with unfulfillable striving and unrelievable restlessness. Insecurity is latent in even the most cohesive of societal relationships; it is open and active where the tissues of trust fail to protect vulnerability, and to support and limit the enjoyment of interests. Suffering of various kinds is built into the condition of separation from God. Individual reckoning is hard to nail down. War is but the most vicious and destructive expression of the underlying problem.

Why Do the Innocent of War Suffer in War?

The problem remains of the different ways of involvement in war by different people and the differing degrees of culpability. Specifically, why do the innocent, the ordinary, the unconnected suffer in war? There is no answer that will satisfy human rationality. Perhaps the explanation just given is closest to the truth: War is a societal phenomenon; as such it sweeps everyone in the society up into its chaos. The innocent suffer with the guilty because they are members together, and sometimes the guilty do not suffer at all. To extend the point theoretically, one can explain the commonality in suffering—guilty and innocent together—by identifying human reality as personhood—an organic, not purely an individual, reality. Society is a set of relationships among persons who are not merely a collection of individuals. We are members one of another. When there is dislocation and

---

3. For an analysis of the problem of collective guilt, see Weber, "Guilt: Yours, Ours, and Theirs."

disorder in one part of the social body, the other members feel it. Even the ones who are most loyal to God are not exempt. In fact, they may be the ones who feel the suffering most acutely. It is not fair, but it is a consequence of being human and of existing as persons in society. God makes the rain to fall on the just and on the unjust.

Or perhaps one can explain it as vicarious suffering. H. Richard Niebuhr has taken this option by explaining unmerited, uninvited suffering in war with the analogy of crucifixion.[4] The crucifixion reveals the reality of vicarious suffering: the suffering of the innocent for the sins of the guilty—not retribution, excuse, or reward. The innocent suffer for the guilty, or more exactly, the weak suffer for the ambitions and excesses of the powerful. The analogy of vicarious suffering is called in because the retribution explanation does not work, and therefore neither does the corollary argument that judgment brings measured and accurate punishment for sins. The cross of Christ discloses the reality of the human situation in war. There is judgment on sin, but the suffering of the innocent and powerless is not a manifestation of judgment. Even this innocent suffering is salvific, however, if it rouses a widespread consciousness of the evil and prods contending societies to move relationships to a more supportive and redemptive level.

I find this analogical use of vicarious suffering intriguing but not sufficient to explain why the innocent suffer when the guilty do not. The analogy is useful in pointing out to us that the innocent do in fact suffer in consequence of someone else's sinful actions. But I am reluctant to call that suffering *vicarious*. The innocent simply suffer, and they suffer because of the misdeeds and mistakes of others, but they do not suffer on their behalf or in place of them. Nor does it help much to suggest that this innocent suffering may be redemptive if it prompts others to better and more responsible behavior. Maybe that will happen, and maybe not. Nevertheless, the use of the analogy may help us understand the reality of relationships without resorting to a literal notion of retribution. It illuminates elements of the human condition uncovered by the symbols of faith, and perhaps not known otherwise. The dislocation manifesting divine judgment entails the unavoidability of innocent and vicarious suffering. Judgment is not expressed as retributive punishment. It is evidence of a deeper malady.

---

4. Niebuhr, "War as Crucifixion." For Niebuhr's views on war, see also Niebuhr, "War as the Judgment of God," and Aldrich and Niebuhr, "Is God in the War?"

My main objection, however, is a theological one. The event of Christ on the cross is a moment in the history of divine salvation. It is not reducible to analogy, and when used as an analogy it loses something of its theological weight. Jesus of Nazareth had a sense of fitting into the divine historical narrative. He surrendered himself, trusting in a God who he thought had forsaken him. By contrast, the innocent sufferers in war simply are caught up and sacrificed.

The Moral Significance of Judgment

What, however, is the moral significance of judgment through war? It is not in signaling individual culpability, but in its function as a call to individual and collective self-criticism, and to confession of sin. If the bad consequences do not identify and nail the perpetrators, neither do those bad consequences allow them to escape into some retreat of self-exoneration and blaming of others. "All have sinned and come short of the glory of God. There is none that is righteous; no, not one!" (Rom 3).

Let us pay special attention to several implications of the context of judgment on all planning and execution of war. First, in the context of judgment on all participants, one may be able to speak of a justified war, but not of just war. Before God all peoples, leaders, and armies are unjust. Particular uses of military force may be justified in accordance with just war criteria, but the notion of what is "just" must be understood in this restricted sense: moral permission to act. Nothing in this particular judgment allows one side to imagine for itself a posture of general moral superiority to the other side. Confession, repentance, and self-correction are mandatory for all participants, and especially for those most certain of the righteousness of what they are doing.

Second, given this context of universal judgment, no participant is entitled to claim divine approval for what it is doing. There is no basis in divine grace for claiming, "God is on our side." No one is entitled to sing "God Bless America" (or bless any other country) if the implication is that this nation is totally free of guilt for the occurrence and calamities of war, and that others therefore can be totally blamed and mercilessly punished. To the contrary, all should confess their sins, act with restraint, and ask forgiveness for what they are doing. Third, there can be no rightful Manichaean division of contending parties into the good and the evil, accompanied by a sense of moral superiority that justifies righteous destruction and punitive reprisals. War cannot "rid the world of evil," especially by destroying the opponent.

Basically, this context of judgment on war is a means of discernment, reminding the human creatures what is required of them to be truly human, but also disclosing to them the impossibility of fulfilling those requirements in any temporal resolutions free of the disordering tendencies they seek to escape. It is a reminder also that no human righteousness can purchase the favor of God, and that there is none to allow any person or party to claim moral superiority and exemption from judgment in the case of war. That is not to say that there are no moral distinctions in the causes and conduct of war. There are—but no party can set itself apart from the need for repentance and forgiveness.

Judgment in the Context of Grace

To return to reflection on H. R. Niebuhr's analogy: this theological recovery suggests other relevant points implied in the analogical use of crucifixion. One is that God suffers in the tragedies and pains of war just as God suffers in the crucifixion of the only Son. God's suffering falls under the judgment of dislocation and disorientation, and at the same time discloses a larger context that encloses judgment and reshapes its meaning. Another is that crucifixion and resurrection belong together, and cannot be separated even to create a useful analogy. What resurrection might mean as an answer to war is a problem for further investigation. It is not, in any event, equivalent to the dawning of an earthly peace in which all conflict and suffering will be overcome. What is clear, however, is that the linking of crucifixion and resurrection is the linking of judgment and grace. Grace is the larger context, and the necessary context, of judgment. The judgment of God in war—whatever it might mean—is not an independent, stand-alone factor. It occurs in the history of divine reconciliation. Divine judgment comes always in the context of divine grace. It is not an unrelieved negation but an instrument of renewal and healing. God intervenes in war not to condemn, reprimand, and destroy but to overcome: "God did not send the Son into the world to condemn the world, but in order that the world might be saved through him" (John 3:17 NRSV). Grace is the means of renewal and new creation. It is the grounds of forgiveness where fellowship and community have been broken. It is the wide context of judgment, the reason why judgment leads to renewal and not simply to destruction.

Preservation

Preservation—as a work of God on behalf of the fallen creation—is a prominent element in the history of Christian political thought. The original biblical narrative of divine preservation appears in the story of the patriarch Noah in the book of Genesis. There God is represented as repenting of having created what turned out to be a wicked race and vowing its total destruction, only to have a change of mind and to propose to rescue some remnant of the people through the instrument of the righteous Noah and his family (Gen 6).

> The LORD saw that the wickedness of humankind was great in the earth, and that every inclination of the thoughts of their hearts was only evil continually. And the LORD was sorry that he had made humankind on the earth. . . . So the LORD said, "I will blot out from the earth the human beings I have created—people together with animals . . . for I am sorry that I have made them." (Gen 6:5–7 NRSV)

A radical solution to what appears to be a divine mistake—a lack of forethought concerning the implications of human freedom. Nevertheless, God decided to preserve humankind through Noah and his family and also the animals he is instructed to bring along on the ark. The reason for relenting is not divine mercy but selective human righteousness and obedience. Noah and his family are chosen for preservation because they are the only righteous ones on the earth, and because Noah walks with God.

Observe the plan of this narrative. The story begins with creation, continues with definitions of human nature and responsibility, and with instructions concerning what is allowed and what not allowed, and next come disobedience and catastrophic consequences. Then follows the divine, "Hm. What have I done? This is terrible! It is not working as I had planned. Better destroy it all, and maybe think of something different!" What happens next introduces preservation almost as an afterthought. God finds a truly righteous man, and because of his godly walk decides to preserve him and his family and representative pairs of animals while destroying all other life. To a social Darwinian this might look like the perpetuation of the species through the survival not of the fittest but of the truly righteous. Of course, it does not work. God does not remove freedom of choice from the fundament of human being, with predictable consequences. Also, the deity acknowledges ruefully that human beings are wicked from the start. And so the narrative must continue to unfold.

In the proposal set forth in the present book, the narrative does not emerge from the beginning. It is read backward from the revelation of God in Christ. The narrative is a comprehensive history of grace, arranged and interpreted from its culmination: the work of God in Christ for the salvation of the world. Preservation is a definite and necessary element in the history of divine grace. It is not an alternative that appears as an option in the course of trying to work out a problem caused by human beings not following God's orders. In the history-of-grace narrative, preservation is an inherent aspect of God's plan and work to renew and reconcile the fallen creation. God intends the redemption of this creation, and holds it in being while the healing work proceeds. This "holding the creation in being" is the preservative element in the history of gracious recovery and renewal. The interpretation is fundamentally christological. Its meanings and transformations derive from the full and final revelation of God in Christ, whose intentions and efforts are for the reconciliation of the *kosmos*. One must understand preservation in the light of this reconciling work, and not simply as a fallback plan for continuing to work with a wayward humanity.

In addition to the distinction drawn already, there are principally two differences between a christological interpretation of preservation and this earlier, non-christological narrative. First, in the Noachian narrative God preserves only a remnant, both of humans and of animals. God's reconciling work in Christ, by contrast, is for the entirety of the fallen creation. Second, God preserves Noah, and by extension his family, because Noah alone is righteous and "walks with God." In the Christian narrative, no one is of sufficient righteousness to deserve anything from God. All humankind is under the power of original sin, and all human beings respond to temptation by committing actual sin. The ground for preservation is the righteousness of Christ, not the righteousness of a few human beings. Justification is the work of God in Christ that extends to all humankind. Therefore the divine intention for preservation extends to everything in the context of saving grace. Justification through the merits of Christ is what allows for preservation. Reconciliation is what requires it. Preservation is not because of merit, but because of "grace, grace, wonderful grace."

Further Contrasting Narratives

Once one leaves the Noachian account of preservation and enters the Christian story there are at least two other alternative guiding and interpretive narratives. Their differences indicate, among other things, how the concept of preservation itself can be extended in meaning by its placement and function in the story. One account already is familiar, because it is the fundamental offering of this book. The entire history of God in relation to the fallen creation is structured in this completed narrative: creation, fall, judgment, preservation, renewal and recovery—read: reconciliation. Reconciliation is the meaning of the whole narrative. It is the active work throughout and the connecting thread in all the elements. Preservation, as I have argued, is an essential element of the history. It is the gracious provision in the totality of the history for sustaining in existence what has fallen. It is one condition of the active presence and continuing work of reconciliation throughout its entire providential course—even, and especially, on the occasion of war. One cannot grasp the meaning of God's work of whole-making through time without acknowledging the sustaining role of preservation therein. Nor can one analyze and proclaim the reality and fullness of preservation without accounting for its embodiment in the reconciling history of grace.

However, there is another way of writing the narrative, especially as it pertains to war and its consequences. In this method, theological thinking about war begins essentially with original sin. The argument is that war has no presence in original creation but enters the picture only with the fall of humankind—the rebellion that rejects the plan and rule of God. From that point on one explains war as originating in sin, having the character of sin, serving to deal with the effects of sin, and at times being justified as punishment for sin. This line of thinking then advances the work of preservation of the fallen creation as the principal (and gracious) mode of divine intervention. The defined means of preservation is government or the state, which organizes the forces of sin against themselves in order to maintain domestic order and protect against external enemies. To carry out these responsibilities, it uses armed force where necessary (and sometimes where not necessary, which is part of the problem). In traditional Lutheran theology, for example, the state is referred to as an *order of preservation*. It is not itself redemptive, but it serves the *order of redemption* not only by supporting the preservative work of God but also, in the view of some, by providing time and space for the proclamation of the Gospel.

JUDGMENT, PRESERVATION, AND HISTORICAL PRESERVATION

The divine plan to control sin by turning sin against itself extends the principle into international relations.[5] The idea is that the conflict among states will generate its own control mechanism, probably in the form of something like a balance of power. Matching self-interest with self-interest and force with force then can be understood as the means God uses to preserve humankind against self-destruction in a sinful world otherwise totally out of control. That is a proposal of some merit, although it works better in some historical situations than in others.

Preservation as a work of God restrains sin by limiting the destructive consequences of war and by maintaining some minimum of life and human association to serve as the basis for the construction of continuing societal order. The preoccupation is with the control of sin, not with a comprehensive concept of the history of grace. Preservation, answering to original sin, remains the focus for theological thinking about war.

This approach is not inherently christological in its fundamental method, although it does incorporate a significant and necessary christological element. That is, even though it is part of the Christian story, it does not interpret the meaning of war and preservation primarily from the work of God in Christ. If there is any connection with redemptive grace it is, as I have said, in the function of preservation in providing time, space, and possibility for the proclamation of the Gospel. Sin to war to preservation to state to order and defense: that describes the narrative with which one talks about divine intervention in this tragic and violent result of human disobedience.

I must mention one other theological attempt to counter radical destruction as the response of God to widespread sin and disobedience. One expects the justice of God to sweep away into oblivion that which was created so lovingly and ideally, but which through disobedience has thoroughly disrupted the divine intention and plan—God's attitude at the beginning of the Noah story, and before the change of mind leading to the building of the ark. In this alternative view, divine mercy intervenes—contrary to expectation—to overrule the severities and strict legality of divine justice. Divine mercy contravenes divine justice. The argument makes the case from an understanding of qualities in the mind and heart of God, and the mystery of how the divine will exercises one in priority over the other. It does not issue in a systematic provision for preservation in the context

---

5. See, for examples, the discussions of state, sin, war, and international politics in Thielicke, *Theological Ethics*, vol. 2, *Politics*.

of a more comprehensive theological vision, by which I mean a framework for connecting the divine work of healing and renewal with the political experiences and institutions. It works with a competition of attitudes toward disappointment and reprisal, and is not of direct use in thinking theologically about war. Therefore it does not provide the material for a political theology.

The two theories that allow us to think theologically about war in comprehensive fashion differ from each other in arguing from the context of grace in one case and from the problem of original sin in the other. Nevertheless, both of them affirm the theological character and necessity of preservation. By doing so, they affirm also the instruments of preservation, especially power and the state. Accordingly, they require us to examine these instruments in the light of their theological and moral parameters. Let us turn therefore to an examination of the problems of power and state as phenomena in themselves, but especially as instruments of preservation in relation to war.

Governmental Power, Its Limits and Tendencies

God's work leading from original creation to the renewal of the fallen creation is the context for understanding governmental power, and indeed all power, in thinking about problems of war and politics. The reality of governmental power, whether fundamental or existential, becomes ultimately intelligible only in the disclosures of that history. This context makes clear that the power of God transcends earthly power in all its forms, defines its ends and limits its applications, and directs that it be confined to its temporal roles. Governmental power is authorized in this context both to restrain and punish sin and to assist in the development of latent and active possibilities in the creation. That is a lot, but that is all. It is temporal power, authorized to pursue and serve only temporal ends. Put somewhat differently, it is secular power, disallowed political objectives serving ends that carry an aura of religious sanctity and a pretension to ultimate solutions of proximate, historical conflicts. It is not tasked with bringing in the kingdom of God or with resolving fundamental problems of good and evil. Governmental power does not fight for the church on the plane of history, nor is it allowed to create Manichaean dualisms or to engage in crusades of messianic deliverance. The temporal-defining and secularizing context requires that states in conflict and their peoples render to Caesar *only* that which is Caesar's, and not ever the things that are God's. It is an application in international politics of the commandment "Thou shalt have no other gods before me." When and where governmental power does not accept this confinement, it must be exposed and resisted.

However, as we know from the actual history of states, governmental power is not inclined to remain within those limits and to accept its role as merely temporal and secular power. This rejection of position and function in the divine ordering is the *hubris* of original sin, human beings expanding in self-importance to displace God—a tendency encouraged and augmented by the possession and experience of collective might. It is also the greater egoism and aggressiveness of groups compared with individuals (Reinhold Niebuhr),[6] the "trend towards unification in the modern state" (Luigi Sturzo),[7] and/or the loss of the sense of transcendence in Western civilization (Eric Voegelin).[8] It is compounded by the emergence of *reason of state* as the final arbiter of international conflict, replacing natural law, international law, and any international institutional means of control. The explanations are theological, psychological, sociological, historical—or all of them together identifying and explaining the divinization of temporal power. That it should happen comes as no surprise when political reality is understood in the context of the divine-human history and its disclosures, especially the Augustinian insight concerning god-making tendencies of persons and states pursuing recovery of meaning through dominance in conflict, and the persistent temptations to make political action in history a saving force. That it does in fact happen is sufficient warning that power can descend or expand into wicked applications and demonic manifestations whatever its beneficial justifications may be.

Comparisons

Up to this point, and given this analysis of power, state, and preservation, one can register extensive agreement between the two theological starting points: original sin and the history of reconciling grace. Both recognize the role of sin in creating the conditions for war (which they agree does not exist in the original plan of God) and in magnifying the pretensions of states in domestic and international politics. Both nominate states as the executors

6. Niebuhr, *Moral Man and Immoral Society*, especially the Introduction, xi–xxv.
7. Sturzo, *Inner Laws of Society*, chapter 11, 269–98.
8. Voegelin, *New Science of Politics*, especially chapter 4, 107–32.

of preservation, and assign them the tasks of maintaining domestic order and providing defense against external enemies. Both recognize power as the instrument of states in discharging these responsibilities. Where then, and why, do they differ, and how do these differences derive from their differing theological starting points?

The differences essentially are in their comparative concepts of power and state. When theological analysis is preoccupied with sin in explaining and dealing with war, it thinks of power primarily as force, the ability to repel the advances of external enemies and to overcome them, and internally the ability to compel compliance by subjects. Similarly, when it begins with original sin as the starting point for thinking of war, it interprets the state mainly with respect to its ordering and defending functions. A state focused on these responsibilities is a relatively complete and contained unit. It is the primary object and occasion of political thought. Other states are external entities and have the same responsibilities. They stay apart, or they cooperate warily and uneasily, or they clash. When they clash, they exert their power against each other. Under these circumstances, power is interpreted mainly as force, not as a combination of force and consent.

By contrast, when theological analysis employs the fullness of the history of grace as its starting point, and not original sin, it invites much more organic and complex thinking about power. Such thinking diversifies power into both consent and force, acknowledging that the two elements appear in different combinations in different times and settings, and allow for—and perhaps demand—different possibilities for action. Beyond the balancing of forces, but not excluding them, it encourages diplomacy, contractual agreements, the codification of laws, the formation of institutions with some provision—surely limited—for authority, and even some degree of trust. Of course, even there it takes full account of the presence and pervasiveness of original sin, but without allowing it to direct the elaboration of thought and possibilities.

Also, if one begins with the context of the history of reconciling grace, power is discovered to be an element of original creation even though corrupted by sin. Power as consent is present in the original plan of God, a point expounded in Thomistic theology with its contention—reflecting Aristotle—that humankind in its primal condition of social organization required supervision, direction, and division of labor. Before the entry of sin into human experience those factors moved easily with the rational consent of the governed. When sin introduced egoism and the corruption of will, the same factors required varying degrees of force to coerce recalcitrant members of the society. Consent to governance was not dead, but neither was it either sufficient or controlling. In the fallen creation, force comes to play a role in power that was not required in original creation.

In the context of reconciling grace, which reveals the plan of God in creation, the state is understood as the institutional form of a political community, an organization of power for pursuit of domestic goods, one of which is public order, and for action in international relations. Its power is understood to be a variable combination of force and consent, and is not equated simply with force. With respect to domestic governing, the leaders and institutions can be pressed more intentionally toward articulation of the internal relationships of the society, bringing more groups and persons into active participation in the common life, and moving the exercise of power more toward consent than force. With respect to war, the state is more capable of imagining relationships not limited fundamentally to relative balances of forces, but open to the forging of associative connections leading to relative peace. That is, it is more capable of such imagination when the theological starting point for an understanding of the state is the history of redemptive grace and not original sin.

Lest the basic point be lost, this insight does not relocate the method of thinking from grace to nature, or original creation. The history of grace reveals to us the content of original creation, but it does so in the discernment of the fundamental essence of creatures and their vocations, not in the exposing of a created order that can be understood in and of itself, and on which grace is superimposed. The creature is viewed differently within history, not as it might have existed before history, or might exist outside of it. This discovery of truth within history is a work of grace, not of clarified reason. Put differently, the allowance or vocation of preservation is grounded not in a natural right of self-defense, but in the larger and longer mission of God to renew and reconcile the fallen creation. In fact, it is not primarily about self-preservation but about the evoking and shaping of organic matrices that extend the preserving conditions much more widely.

Does it therefore imply another and higher institutional level, something on the order of a world government, subordinating the power of states to its own jurisdiction and control, focusing all efforts beyond the states on international common interests and creating temporal conditions for the elimination of war? Certainly it opens the way to something mutually more agreeable and profitable than a balance of military forces. But any such projections beyond the states are limited in their prospects by the persistence of sin and its effects, as well as by the practical problems of differentials in size, history, and culture and the dispersion of populations across the globe. The history of grace as context, by contrast with original sin, invites organic possibilities of cooperation and institutionalization beyond the level of the state system, although it does not support the promise of an integral world government. International organizations are welcomed and encouraged in this context, and they may help mitigate conflict and promote cooperation, but they are not the way of salvation from war. The issue at this point is preservation moving by grace and responsive human effort toward a more civilizing combination of consent with force, but not a deliverance from all conflict within historical experience.

War self-evidently is an instrument of destruction, but in the course of its history pressures arise to restrict, neutralize, or defeat the pressures to destroy that are inherent in war. One may list these pressures under the heading of preservation. Preservation is an effort to answer destruction, although it does so unevenly and not always with a lot of success. However, to repeat the governing claim, preservation does not stand alone as a value or reality or system of meaning. It is an element in the original and ongoing work of redemption. In this respect the *ordering of preservation* is inherent in the work of the *ordering of redemption*, even though the functions and contributions of state and church remain different.

A Binding Concern

These two theories not only agree that preservation is the intention of God; they make that element essential to God's activity in providing for the fallen creation. It follows that concern for preservation is binding on Christian responses to war and cannot be shucked off with the claim that only ultimate redemption is of interest to God. Preservation is a principled concern in theological thinking about war. However, the specific details of preservation do not follow immediately from the concept itself, but must be left to the context of conflict. That is, commitment to the principle of preservation does not imply directly and explicitly the preservation of London or Beijing, or the *Mona Lisa* or the Egyptian pyramids, or Wembley Stadium in England or Tiger Stadium in Baton Rouge. As a principle preservation is tested in its ability to limit and overcome war, given the proclivity of war to destroy much of what it touches. It enters war not as a focused choice for preserving particulars but as a divine mandate to limit and to overcome. It finds its real efficacy in the promotion of peace, which is the next and preservative step in the organization of power.

The Possibilities of History

Now we must ask whether history allows the possibility that wars can be avoided, or at least restrained and limited, or maybe even eliminated altogether from human experience. Is human history in the context of grace totally open to such possibilities, or do the dislocations to which grace responds close out any such openness? The short answers are, first, that human history never will see the total end either of conflict in human experience or of territorial divisions of some kind in international society. Therefore it always will include the possibility of war. Proposals for total world peace without end may have some value for critiquing the present and imagining the future, but they do not eliminate the need to deal with the rough stuff of power, consent, and enforcement. Second, no particular war is necessary, and none is mandated by fate to be conducted or to end in a predetermined way. Efforts to promote peace indeed can have some relevance and effective influence. One should never dismiss or abandon such efforts, even though the future is not as hopeful as we might like and the prospects for change are not warmly encouraging.

Why such pessimism with regard to the abolition of war? The governing explanation is theological. The wars of human history, whatever their experiential "causes," reflect the fundamental disruption in existence produced by human rejection of sole dependence on God. Once that discernment is in place, we cannot avoid the conclusion that the prospect of conflict—including its maximum expression in war—will not be eliminated from human history so long as this disruption remains in force. There will be the potential for war, if not the actuality of it, unless and until all human beings are reunited with God. Continuing territorial divisions across the world provide the occasions, even if not the fundamental dynamic. The further conclusion is that even if this restoration with God is possible, it is not possible by the will of human beings. To follow the Augustinian analysis once again, the will is in bondage to sin and cannot free itself to return to its validating and authenticating relationship. There is no rescue except by divine grace, and that, of course, is what the history of God's reconciling work is all about. However, the conclusion and consummation of that work is not a prospective event in human history. It is an eschatological event. It will occur only when the Lord returns to straighten everything out, or more appropriately, to make all things new. Until then, conflict will persist in human experience, and with it, the possibility of war.

What this means is that none of the grand schemes for historical transformation will produce final, beneficent transformations, however inspired and compelling they may seem to their proponents. There will be no elimination of quarrels and fights through class struggle synthesizing into a classless society; no "end of history" with democratic government and liberal capitalism as the only imaginable alternatives;[9] no threat-removing hegemony or completion of imperial rule; no liberal democratic international order of law and government resolving all human rights complaints and all conflicts of states; no messianic reordering of world power into conformity with an ideal religious prophecy; no liberation that does not require a new order of power; no Muslim *umma* enfolding all of the world's peoples. This is not to say that all of these proposals are totally wrong and that nothing can be learned from them. It is to say, however, that they will produce only a different arrangement of goods and power, perhaps better, perhaps worse, but presupposing the continuing disruption of the divine-human relationship. No historical salvation. No final termination of conflict and its manifestations.

But that is not all there is to say about historical possibility. Even granting that history is closed to the total elimination of conflict and wars from human experience, it is not closed absolutely, and the events of history do not move according to predetermined causation. Much can be done through the imagining of futures different from the present or prospective ones and the efforts to realize them within the limits of that experience. To begin with, the relative openness of history shows us, as I have stated, that particular wars do not have to happen, however inevitable they may seem to be. Decisions taken with regard to definition of interests, development of material resources, threats of action, and demands on others may seem to impose on states an iron-bound course toward war, but no outcome is so predetermined that it cannot be deflected by some combination of human reason and will, with some elements of luck and accident. Particular wars are avoidable. Their prospective avoidance is good reason for energetic peacemaking and diplomatic negotiations.

9. The allusion is to an argument advanced by Francis Fukuyama, but later modified by him in *The End of History and the Last Man*.

What makes that so? Simply put, it is the ambiguity of human nature, even in the creatures who suffer the radical disruption of separation from God. One part of the ambiguity is, of course, the persistence of the "bent to sinning," to use Charles Wesley's term. The other, however, is the residual capacity for transcendence, which allows some freedom both in imagining arrangements of power different from existing ones and in acting to move from one condition to the other. The continuing force of the sinful will forecasts some degree of corruption of the transcendent vision and of the program of action, and the inability to move out of one's position in time and space distorts the broader view, but neither of these factors nor their combination eliminates some degree of freedom to pry open the historical futures.

If ambiguity is present in disrupted human nature, so also is it found in the arrangements of political history. Some long-standing problems are resolved in history, old enemies sometimes come together in embracing institutions and cooperative ventures, and international bodies take charge of the management of some issues over which states formerly fought. All this (usually) is to the good. But new conflicts arise, dormant power becomes aggressive, states divide into competing segments, some of them fail and become power vacuums in the international system, economic dislocations provoke political disputes, and nonstatal forces emerge on the historical scene to drive their own seemingly eccentric and arbitrary programs. The historical pattern is one of integration and disintegration. It persists, and with it the relative openness of political futures and the ambiguity of historical results.

What, then, are we left with—in terms of historical expectations to serve as basis or at least parameters for policy planning? Are we back to the classical realist scenario: states expanding their power, bumping into other states doing the same, and achieving a balance of sorts that allows them to live in "peace" for awhile, at least until the next major dislocation? Certainly there will be persistent elements of these power realities in international experience, but there are other considerations. One is that—contrary to traditional *realpolitische* theory—expansion of power is not a permanent energizer and director of state behavior. Some states achieve a relatively high level of satisfaction with their status, and do not drive for significant revisions of inter-state relationships.[10] Another is that the states may engage

---

10. A compelling revision of the realist proposal, by someone in important respects in the realist tradition, is Arnold Wolfers' *Discord and Collaboration*. Wolfers points out that some states in the international system are relatively satisfied with what they have

in the process of the *civilization of power*—a transformation of power from heavy reliance on force to predominance of consent (to be described more fully in a later chapter), often with the reciprocity of power institutionalized into international law and organization. The underlying dynamic remains, because the ambiguity of human nature does not change. Relatively mature integration of international society can descend to aggressive disintegration. The foundations of a promising international order can shake once again. There is no guarantee of permanence, no certain freedom from possibilities of war, no political deliverance in experienced history. But some openness to historical possibility remains, and with it some limited opportunities to shape the future.

The mandate of faith seeking peace is that one should seize those opportunities, or create them. For example, one should study carefully the proposals for "just peacemaking" in books on that topic written or edited by Glenn H. Stassen.[11] The premise of these proposals, as I understand it, is that in any given case the march toward conflict is not inexorable. Change is possible. Wars may be avoidable, or at least their destructive consequences may be mitigated. Ethical thinking about such wars should not be limited to questions of justification, that is, to whether no war is ever justified (absolute pacifism), or whether justification may be recognized when the proposed action meets certain specified tests (just war ethic). Instead, it should exploit the openings of history in these particular cases, or seek to create them where they do not exist, by activating and pursuing relevant peacemaking initiatives. Persons of conscience and competence should disengage both from particularistic loyalties and from despair over practical

---

and do not entertain goals that lead them to behave aggressively. Other states have more ambitious goals, and therefore seek to spread their reach and influence—often forcibly. Relationships among the former are characterized by amity, the latter by enmity. States in historical existence are arranged more or less on an "amity-enmity" spectrum, a dynamic positioning from which states can move in one direction or another along the line. Those states enjoying relative satisfaction, or simply wanting to avoid war, can project policies to move them toward the "amity" end of the spectrum. In doing so, they can encourage institutional and legal developments that will leave them less dependent on the maximization of national power. Those states that are dissatisfied, and those that simply want to flex their muscles and take what is not theirs, will provoke fights and move toward the "enmity" end. See especially chapter 2, "Amity and Enmity among Nations."

11. Stassen, *Just Peacemaking: Transforming Initiatives for Justice and Peace*; Stassen, *Just Peacemaking: Ten Practices for Abolishing War*. The subtitle reference to "abolishing war" goes beyond what I believe to be theologically and practically achievable, but the efforts to avoid particular wars, reduce their likelihood, and promote justice certainly are defensible and to be encouraged.

possibilities of change, and seize upon and execute wise and appropriate methods to press for responsible dispositions of power.

One should face the fact that contributions to peace are made by observing and analyzing the ways that power relations are contrived in the milieu of conflict and cooperation, by imagining different constructions of those relations, and by working to shape the best outcomes imagined as alternatives to war. Although one can and must project outcomes different from the threatening future, one nevertheless must work from the present reality, and not from idealistic dreams of a future disconnected from the present. To publish visions of world peace unrelated to what actually is happening is not as helpful as the proponents suppose, and these visions are not likely to be taken seriously by those who actually make decisions. That is why the "just peacemaking" proposals are much more likely to make peace. And of course, there is no theological support for crusades in the name of God to destroy the disturbers of God's peace by simply eliminating them, and no basis for Manichaeanism, for designating combatants as purely good on one side and purely evil on the other, with the corollary implication that the good are both ordained and empowered to purify and sanctify the world by destroying those who are evil. There is no salvation within history, at least in the sense that attractive uses of power can resolve once and for all the temptations and abuses of power. Neither the imposition of power through war nor the renunciation of power to avoid war is salvific. But particular wars can be avoided and new structures of cooperation can be created by embracing and employing the possibilities afforded in the relative openness of history.

The history of grace tells us that there is no salvation of history itself by historical means. As a critical principle it negates the claims of the grand, salvific schemes and programs, reducing their appeals to more material elements of conflict. It exposes also the divinizing tendencies of nationalistic sentiments in war, separating the calls of ordinary patriotism and legitimate defense from the glories of death in battle and the self-congratulation of triumph. Those are not small contributions to the limitation and transformation of war. To them we must add the revelation of true humanity as image of God and the common responsibility to care for the earth. These disclosures denounce the restriction of true humanity to members of one's own "tribe," so-called, and the consequent vilification and dehumanization of others "not of our kind." The common responsibility, to which I referred, rejects wars of imperialism as well as more limited war aims to claim territories merely to support national interests—political, economic, religious.

The more comprehensive project of God's reconciling activity in this history is to encourage the formations of power away from dominant expressions of force to greater reliance on consent, with the fields of consent reaching beyond national boundary and consciousness to shape community as an international reality. It is the vision for placing judgment in the context of repentance and forgiveness, and shaping preservation toward more inclusive relationships and not only toward protecting what is one's own. It is a call for politics to enter the reconciling activity and be motivated and formed by it, and not merely by belligerence, aggrandizement, and self-interest. These contributions from the history of gracious divine activity are discernments of faith, not reports from experience and empirical study. They are insights into the reality of war from theological inquiry.

PART TWO
The Political Context

6

War in the Context of Politics

Limitations on the extreme logic of war are established in the first place—and perhaps in the final place—by locating war in the context of politics. By the same movement, one also creates the possibilities of conversation between war and reconciliation. To see what is meant in a fundamental sense by locating war in the context of politics, let us extend our reading of the Prussian officer and military theorist Carl von Clausewitz. That will allow us to trace the movement from politics to war and back to politics. With that understanding in place, we shall have the framework and organic substance in place for eventually engaging the contrasting logic of reconciliation.

Extending Clausewitz: War and *Politik*

In an earlier chapter I argued that Clausewitz's stark portrayal of the logic of war as unrelenting and unlimited violence was qualified by him in two ways. First, he distinguished between absolute or theoretical war and real war, the point being that in actual conflict numerous factors intervened to prevent the absolute logic of war from being determinative of its conduct. Second, he subordinated war to politics—a limitation of variable but usually decisive effect. Here we pick up on and extend the second of these two qualifications.

Clausewitz's famous and oft-quoted saying, repeated several times in his celebrated work *On War*, is, "War is the continuation of *Politik* by other means." I have used the German word *Politik* quite deliberately, because it can be translated as "policy" and as "politics." Clausewitz used both meanings to explain war. War is a continuation of policy, because it is an instrument called into service when other means of achieving policy objectives fail, or as an implicit threat. War serves a political object, with reference to which both its strategy and its tactics are judged. Absent this politically instrumental character, war makes absolutely no sense. It is simply an exercise of unrestrained violence. It loses any pretense to justification and becomes merely an irrational act. And war also is a continuation of politics, in the sense of ongoing political intercourse with the domestic public, with allies, and even with enemies while the war proceeds.

> We know . . . that war originates through the political intercourse of governments and nations, but it is generally supposed that such intercourse is terminated by war, and that a totally different state of things ensues, subject to no laws but its own. We maintain, on the contrary, that war is nothing but a continuation of political intercourse with an admixture of other means. . . . This political intercourse does not cease through the war itself.[1]

It is clear from both of Clausewitz's meanings of *Politik* that war exists and operates in the context of politics, and that it must be understood in and through that context.[2] War continues policy as its instrument, and also in the political interaction among parties engaged in the conflict. In this extended and comprehensive political context one can see a line of progression: from pre- to post-war, wherein war is the central element in the political process without ever leaving it.

Politics to War to Politics

As I have argued, Clausewitz initially examined the institution of war as an abstraction, separating it out from surrounding social reality in order to identify its essence, namely, the logic of violence. However, as soon as he left the realm of abstraction and turned to war's actual context of social reality, he spoke of war as a "continuation of *Politik* by other means." The true home of war, and therefore the framework for understanding it, is *die Politik*, understood both as policy and as politics. This contextualization in politics enables us to sketch a sequence of relationships in the course of conflict: it is politics to war; politics during war (or the politics of war); the

---

1. Clausewitz, *War, Politics, and Power*, 255.
2. See chapter 2, n. 4, for a comment stating that Jean Bethke Elshtain set forth only the absolutist side of Clausewitz's understanding of war.

return from war to politics.³ In this scheme as in reality, war is not an event, separate unto itself. It is a jarring and disruptive but connected element of a political process.

Broken down into its elements, the scheme looks like this: First, from *politics to war* (without really leaving politics). War is an instrument of national policy. It is one of several means by which states pursue their policies and political objectives—whether these are judged to be good or bad, justified or unjustified. The primary approach should be for states to use means other than force, especially diplomacy, to serve these policies and objectives. But if they do resort to military force to pursue unrequited interests, this usage nonetheless is a continuation of politics—by other means. Of course, states may elect to modify, delay, or abandon their interests—in other words, to make different political decisions.⁴ Even so, force may be more or less in the background as threat or as element in the prestige of power. In those cases, the unspoken prospect of war is part of the political process. This point is especially important, because it tells us that military force always is present—practically or theoretically—in the means of power available to states for the pursuit of their interests. They may elect to develop the capability or not to develop it, and in the former case to develop it minimally or maximally. In terms of Wolfers' "amity-enmity" scale, they may regard their military capability as irrelevant in dealing with friendly states but as forward and threatening in dealing with hostile ones.⁵ Weak states may rely, at least implicitly, on the military power of other states or international institutions. Military capability is an aspect of politics; it is neither nonpolitical nor extrapolitical. If politics by nonmilitary means fails, and the state resorts to war, that eventuality is politics by another means, but it is still politics. We revisit Clausewitz: war is a continuation of politics by other means.

Second: *politics during war*. The resort to war is a *continuation* of politics, in several dimensions. One is the relationship of the government to its domestic constituencies. The "Powell Doctrine," so-called, was not the

---

3. I explored the relationship of "politics to war to politics" for the first time in *Modern War and the Pursuit of Peace*.

4. I am using "interest" in a general sense, to allow for values and objectives more inclusive than traditional material, i.e., defense, territorial, and economic interests. Robert Cooper argues for a broader interpretation of the aims of foreign policy in *The Breaking of Nations*, 147–48.

5. See Wolfers, *Discord and Collaboration*, chapter 2, "Amity and Enmity among Nations."

first occasion of a high-level official insisting that going to war, even for a compelling objective, requires the support of the folks at home. Eliciting and maintaining that support is an exercise in politics. The requirement of domestic support might seem less weighty for authoritarian or absolutist governments than for democratically supported ones, for the traditional wisdom concerning the former is that they can disregard popular feelings and do what they want in foreign affairs. However, even tyrants have to watch their backs to be sure no one else in the circle of power uses the war as an occasion to dislodge them. Moreover, authoritarian governments have been known to use the threat of foreign enemies—and even the resort to war—to maintain power at home. And so war may be a continuation even of domestic politics. There is politics during the war, and it is the politics of war.

Another dimension of politics during war is alliance politics—recruiting partners for the fight and keeping them on board. Of course, alliance politics begins before any war—sometimes long before. Usually it defines a common enemy, specifies under what conditions an ally should enter combat on the side of the party with which it has made alliance, what its commitments and responsibilities in the conflict are, and under what conditions it may terminate the alliance and exit the conflict. Alliance politics during the war focuses on keeping allies true to their commitments throughout, thereby assuring that all of the resources on hand or projected before entering the war will be reliably available as the war proceeds. War involves, among other considerations, the continuing and nurturing of alliance politics, especially the building of trust and predictability.

Yet another dimension is relationships with other states and other elements in the international system not involved in the struggle, or not directly involved but uneasy about how this conflict affects them, whether they should get in or stay out, or even whether they should trade with one side or the other. When these two dimensions are entangled with international institutions, such as NATO or the United Nations, those connections often involve the politics of authorization for the uses of military power. (Recall in this regard the unsuccessful efforts of the George W. Bush administration to get authorization from the U.N. for the attack on Iraq in 2003.) And then of course one must acknowledge also the persistent politics of dealing with adversaries. Clausewitz certainly was correct in observing that adversarial relations do not simply break away from political dealings and replace them altogether with overt and unrelenting hostility, even when diplomacy gives way to war. States at war usually attempt to maintain connections with opponents, usually through neutral states or by way of "back channel" contacts. These considerations are further evidence that war itself continues in the political process.[6]

Third: *from war back to politics*. This point is not an admission that war after all is not political. Rather, it refers to the change in political means and objectives from the attempt to subdue the opponent by military force, to the politics of diplomacy and other nonmilitary means and the reconstituting of relationships with more of the character of an emerging civil society. Stated differently, the politics of war moves toward the politics of peace. The process transcends war, but it is not a new departure radically different from the politics of combat, military decisions, conflicts of interest and influence, and power balances, even as it moves toward some sort of resolution. Peace—as we shall see later—is a particular organization of power. The actual organization that results from the process may not fit some ideal notions of "peace," nor is it simply discontinuous from the struggle out of which it emerges, but it will represent the new political reality now becoming the subject matter of any intended or possible revisions. However that peace may be defined, and whatever degree and kind of force may be a component of the new construction, politics of some sort will be the constitutive reality of the reconstituted relationship.

All of these points of analysis confirm the observation that the full course of events must be understood as politics to war/politics, and then back from war to politics. That is the comprehensive picture of war as a continuation of politics by other means.[7] The picture makes clear that war never leaves the context of politics, even though it may change form and relationships within it.

---

6. See Ross, *Statecraft—and How to Restore America's Standing in the World.*

7. My argument, including the extended interpretation of Clausewitz, is very similar to that of Helmut Thielicke in *Theological Ethics*, vol. 2, *Politics*. He writes, "War is something which, in the view of von Clausewitz, has its origin in politics, is a continuation of politics in another medium, and finally leads back to politics" (422). For Thielicke, war is an emergency measure of the state functioning as an order of preservation. He thinks primarily of the war-politics connection with reference to the teleology of *Staatspolitik*, that is, to how the state pursues its interests in international relations. He is less attentive to the more inclusive context of politics, nor does he explore the implications of the state as emergency institution of the order of preservation positioned in the context of reconciliation.

WAR, PEACE, AND RECONCILIATION: PART TWO

The Preeminence of Politics

A premise of the preceding analysis is that in the relationship between the two, politics is predominant over military force and considerations, and must remain so. This is true because military force is an instrument of policy (and therefore not self-justifying), because political objectives must control the use of military force during the course of the war, and because the consolidation of the outcome requires a work of political reconstruction. Often in the course of the war in Iraq since March 2003, and also in Afghanistan, we have heard the observation, "The conclusion of this mess requires a political solution, not a military solution." The point is that political objectives for which military force is the instrument will not be achieved until there is significant reconstitution of the organic, structural, and material substance of the society. The solution requires the creation and strengthening of local and national institutions, the provision of basic services, and the resolution—or at least mitigating—of enduring conflicts among major segments of the population. These issues are political. They are works of political construction, not the predictable fruit of military victory. Any state contemplating war must be fully aware of these political requirements of peace. They are part of the calculation of anticipated costs in justifying resort to war. If the projected costs of peace are too high, they may dictate a decision not to go to war, even if the cause is justified. The point once again is that political considerations, comprehensively understood, trump military considerations, and political control must remain preeminent over the military instrument.

General Douglas MacArthur once famously declared that "in war there is no substitute for victory." The statement seems self-evidently true, especially to persons directly engaged in the fighting. It is potentially a powerful criticism of any policies that hold warriors back from achieving goals toward which their generals direct them. In fact it is not true in all cases and without qualification. What is true is that in war there is no substitute for achieving political objectives. Achieving those objectives may indeed require all-out victory, but they may be gained in some conflicts in a stalemate with compromises, or—preferably—with no combat at all, even if with a threat of force. The overriding consideration is the political objective, not the military domination of the opponent. This point is supported in a somewhat different way from ancient Chinese military wisdom:

"When you do battle, it is necessary to kill people, so it is best to win without fighting."[8]

Commander in Chief

In many societies this relationship of *Politik* to the state's military arm is institutionalized through the primacy of political leaders over military leaders and their subordinates. In the United States of America the relationship is institutionalized in the role of the president as commander in chief of the armed forces of the United States. Article II, Section 2 of the U.S. Constitution states, "The President shall be commander in chief of the Army and Navy of the United States, and of the militia of the several states, when called into the actual service of the United States . . ." The Constitution itself provides no substantive definition of the role beyond that bare statement. It should come as no surprise, therefore, that there has been and continues to be some confusion and disagreement over what the role actually entails and how the president and the military forces of the country are to relate to each other. The temptation—and at times the tendency—is to think of commander in chief primarily in military terms, to imagine the president in times of war or threat of war as the first soldier of the nation, and therefore to regard previous military service as an important and perhaps essential qualification for the job. These assumptions were prominent in the U.S. presidential campaign of 2008, which pitted Senator John McCain, a man with a long, honorable, and at times painful service as a naval officer, against Senator Barack Obama, who could offer no record of military service at all.

In fact, the assumptions are incorrect. Commander in chief is a political office, not a military office. The intent is to establish the authority of the political leaders of the country over the military leaders and their respective commands. A state's military forces exist only to serve the interests of the state. It is the responsibility of the civilian leaders to define the interests, formulate appropriate policies, and select, arrange, and support those instruments of policy that best serve the political ends. Certainly the president must be advised by military leaders as to the military feasibility and costs of certain objectives, as well as the procedures and necessities for the actual uses of military power, and should not make tactical military decisions. But that is not the same as expecting or allowing military

8. Quoted in Sun Tzu, *Art of War*, 67.

leaders to define and promote the larger objectives of the use of force. The U.S. Constitution assigns several roles and functions to the president, only one of which is commander in chief. One should gain an understanding of that role by starting with a comprehensive understanding of the presidency, not by moving up the chain of command until one arrives at the militarily defined top. The president is the chief executive—a civilian officer. He or she is not a six-star general.[9]

Moreover, the primary qualification of the office is political judgment, not military judgment. Previous military experience may be useful, but it is not necessary. Woodrow Wilson and Franklin Roosevelt, who led the country through the two great wars of the twentieth century, did not serve in the military. Abraham Lincoln's military experience was miniscule: he served three very short enlistments in the Illinois state militia during the Black Hawk War. One should add that if a president, by reason of extensive military experience, thinks of foreign policy primarily in military terms, that inclination is likely to be a disservice to the country. It is a point of disqualification for the role of commander in chief.

Derangement of the Powers

Derangement in the proper relationship of the powers occurs when the military arm of the state establishes itself in superiority over the civilian leadership. One pattern of derangement is the intervention of the military leadership in domestic politics to restore a constitutional order that it believes has been compromised if not destroyed by the politicians. The role of the military in Turkish politics is a case in point. The Turkish military restrains itself from a political role except where it believes the government has strayed too far from the pattern established by Kemal Atatürk, founder of the Turkish Republic and its first president. Its primary concern is to maintain the secularity of the state against the prospect of a sharp turn toward Islamic religiosity. The idea is that when the military intervention has performed the work of restoration, the leaders order their soldiers back to the barracks. In such cases, not surprisingly, the military sees its own action not as derangement but as restoring the proper constitutional order. The derangement, in its view, is caused by the civilian leaders, not by the

---

9. Normally the persons of highest military rank wear four stars. In World War II, a few generals and admirals of unusual prominence and responsibility were awarded five stars. Hence the reference to the president not being a "six-star general."

military. The intervention is a temporary, emergency measure, because the military leaders understand themselves and their forces as subordinate to the constitution and the constitutional officers. The ultimate test, of course, is whether the military leaders and their forces in fact restore civilian control and return to their subordinate status.

Another pattern is the outright seizure of power by some faction of the military or one of its prominent leaders. When this happens, the new leadership at the center of power will politicize its role by creating new and subservient institutions and by arranging devices—such as rigged elections, symbols of status and acceptance, and recognition by other states—to legitimate its control. General Pervez Musharraf made himself the dominant force in Pakistan by military seizure of power. He sought to create a new politics of Pakistan, centered around himself and under his control, by among other things removing and replacing the justices of the Supreme Court and establishing a close relationship with the president of the United States. Since his removal from power the civilian government of Pakistan has struggled to establish its authority and control over the Pakistani military and intelligence services, which in important respects remain independent and indeed predominant centers of power within the society.

A third pattern appears when, given inviting circumstances, military leaders are tempted to reverse the order of priority for what they take to be very good reasons. During the Korean War in the early 1950s, the aforementioned General Douglas MacArthur attempted to wrest control of East Asian policy from President Harry Truman by pressuring for more aggressive military action not only on the Korean Peninsula but also with regard to China. MacArthur was contemptuous of Truman, and did not appear to think highly of the presidency itself, by comparison with his own exalted military status. Truman responded by firing MacArthur. It was a bold and controversial move, because MacArthur was enormously popular and the president was held in low esteem by much of the country and was trashed by the Republicans. But Truman did the right thing. He restored the proper relationship of civilian and military leadership, and avoided an even worse political and military disaster than actually was happening.

The authority of civilian over military leadership in domestic society is an inherently precarious relationship, because the military establishment is the repository of force and because military figures at times are more popular and more trusted than their civilian superiors. Civilian control depends on public consent to the exercise of power rooted deeply in tradition and a conscious—or even pre-conscious—acceptance of the right order of power relationships.

The lesson here is that the maintenance of civilian control depends on the strength of the public institutions and their continuing and conscious maintenance. It is important for the president to have popular support for his person and for his efforts to maintain this relationship, but such support may not be adequate if a visible and charismatic military leader is more popular and more trusted than the president. What counts ultimately is the validation of the institutions themselves in the consciousness and historical sense of the people. Part of the institutional fabric is the existence and persistence of a military culture that affirms the relationship. The unpopular President Truman acted on and enforced the constitutional provision as well as the particular element of military culture. Some members of the opposition party were so outraged that they demanded Truman's impeachment. Whether Truman was right in his foreign policy judgment is another matter. What is important to the argument here is that he acted as commander in chief, resisting any degree of derangement in the relationships of civilian and military power. The public as a whole (and most of the political opposition) eventually came to recognize that on that point he was right. The popular general sought his political party's nomination for the presidency, and lost.[10]

Everything Else in Connection with Military Power

I have been following the lead of Thomas Barnett in looking at war in "the context of everything else," principally the context of politics. Following that line, I have argued for the subordination of the military instrument of power to political leadership, institutions, and objectives. However, there is another way to think about the context of everything else, and

10. Bob Woodward reports two occasions on which James Schlesinger, as secretary of defense, disobeyed direct commands by President Gerald Ford. Ford commanded him to send helicopters to evacuate friendly Vietnamese during the fall of Saigon, and also to bomb Cambodia following the SS *Mayaguez* incident. Schlesinger disagreed on both points and refused to carry out the orders, leaving the president to discover later that he had been disobeyed. Schlesinger should have resigned rather than disobey a direct order. Ford should have fired him, but did not, preferring to avoid confrontation. Truman, as commander in chief, surely would have dismissed the secretary, thereby reversing the derangement of powers. Woodward, *Shadow*, 30–31. By contrast with Schlesinger, Secretary of State Cyrus Vance resigned his post rather than support President Jimmy Carter's plan to liberate by invasive force captive U.S. embassy employees in Iran.

that is by beginning with the military instrument and looking at the ways in which it develops an ecology centered on itself. That topic is too broad and complicated to be explored adequately here, but one can at minimum sketch out some of the details. President Eisenhower, himself a five-star general, famously warned of the sinister and far-reaching power of the "military-industrial complex"—an acknowledgment from the top of how deeply integrated are the military establishment and the economic system of the country, with broad implications for public expenditures, political influence, and even political-military decisions.[11] Whenever the Pentagon orders the closing of military bases or defense plants, the members of Congress from the affected states protest immediately. They argue up front that the closings diminish defense capabilities, but their primary concern is that the closings mean loss of jobs, and if the politicians do not resist these moves it means loss of votes. Furthermore, military bases are so closely integrated with their neighboring communities, and contribute so much to their development, that the closing of bases or significant shifts of military personnel can have a devastating effect on the economic base and societal health of the communities. Military enlistment offers employment opportunity and possible career commitment for young people who have trouble finding their places in society. Military culture and careers are themselves societal phenomena that connect well beyond the instrumental implications of military power.

One could give many more examples, but that is not necessary. War and the means of war connect to everything else, and engage in reciprocal influence. Society is built up and deflated by military moves. Economic power and political power come into play. Lives and families by the thousands and millions are influenced. Propaganda and protests flourish. Reconciliation at the societal level is very much at issue, because the role of the military in society involves the health and wholeness of society, its goals and values, and the lives, futures, and relationships of its people.

Reconciliation and War: The Organic Political Context

The engagement of reconciliation with war is through the media of politics and social reality, not immediately with the logic of violence and destruction. Of course, reconciliation must concern itself with violence, its limits and its redirection—as does politics. But the approach to the problem of

11. See Bacevich, "The Tyranny of Defense Inc."

war is by way of institutions, law, the formation of community, the development of possibilities of communication, the eliciting of practices of civility in language and behavior. These societal elements manifest the organic reality of politics as the matrix of war. The work of reconciliation is to maintain and deepen the strength of these forms of social fabric in their role of disciplining the absolutist tendencies of martial violence described by Clausewitz, thereby supporting the control of political office and judgment over military office and judgment, and confining war to its only proper function, that is, as a continuation of politics by other means.

Confining war to its instrumental role does not render it harmless. The political purposes of states worked out by means of war may be grandiose in aims and catastrophic in effects. To control the purposes and means of war requires a steady and committed application of the just war criteria governing resort to the use of this instrument and moral limitation of its means. However, as any student of the problem knows, the force of the just war ethic depends on the good will of states applying it where they act as judges in their own cases. It depends also, in part, on its embodiment in an international ethos accepted by all parties to the contest. Neither of these restraints inspires confidence, especially the latter, at a time when the international ethos itself is repudiated and assaulted by terrorists, so-called rogue states, and prominent religions.

That reservation requires attention to the larger political context of the international system. Clausewitz thought about the political instrumentality of war primarily from the standpoint of the nation-state in conflict with other states. The European state system of his time provided significant limits to resort to war, but it also created temptations to use war to pursue state interests—including the rearrangement of the system itself. Now the international system has expanded to global inclusiveness. It is necessary therefore to look beyond the theoretical analysis of the relationships of war and politics to inquire into the implications for war of the global political system. However, before we consider that system and its relation to our project, we must examine the meanings of power.

7

The Meanings and Problems of Power

When we speak of politics we are dealing, of course, with the realities of power. Power seems to imply coercion, and in that respect puts politics already at odds with reconciliation. When we move then to consider war as an instrument of politics, we discern even sharper antipathy between politics and reconciliation, for power in war implies forcible defense, efforts to dominate and even destroy an opponent, and therefore destruction and killing. And when we declare that any imaginable earthly peace is a particular organization of power, we seem to have moved reconciliation out of the realm of discourse and into a private and interpersonal world. Are we not back to our earlier portrayal of a fundamental and insurmountable contradiction between war and reconciliation?

If there is any way past this contradiction it requires a reconsideration of the nature and role of power. We can do that in terms that are theological on the one hand and nontheological on the other. As to the first possibility, we must recall the place of preservation in the work of God to sustain and renew the fallen creation. God does not destroy humankind as punishment for its wickedness but holds it in being through all its perversions and tribulations to the end of forming a new creation. Holding the world in being requires preservation. Preservation involves power. Power therefore plays an important role in the reconciling work of God. As to the second possibility, we must analyze the nature of power more fully, not allowing it to be equated simply with coercion or force. We shall do that directly in this chapter, and follow the analysis with a distinction between substantial and relational power. Those efforts will allow us to move in later chapters to consideration of the civilizing of power and the necessities and possibilities of understanding peace as an organization of power.

Power as Force and Consent

Perhaps the principal conceptual difficulty with power as a political means, and with peace as an organization of power, derives from the tendency to equate power with force. The notion of "power politics," which pertains mainly to the state system and balance-of-power politics deriving from the Peace of Westphalia (1648), suggests the muscling of states by each other mainly in terms of military threats and actions. In the effort to move away from that understanding, and to open the concept of power to its actual diversity, I define power here as a variable and fluid combination of force and consent. It is variable, because either force or consent may be preponderant—or they may be in relative balance—in any particular organization of power. Power may be simply the imposition of will of the stronger party over the weaker. Or it may embody significant consent to the exercise of leadership and control. In the former case peace is established by maximum and unqualified force, in the latter by widespread agreement to the arrangement based on acknowledgment and protection of interests, rights, and traditions, and participation by all parties in the processes of governance. It is fluid, because the relationships can change—sometimes dramatically—with time and circumstance. One can argue with support from history that sheer force will not maintain a lasting peace unless degrees of consent emerge based on rights and interests respected and justice done, or that a consensual arrangement will not hold together unless there is some central and effective mechanism for judgment, decision, and implementation. That is true enough, but it does not change the fact that peace in one form or another—in a moment or across a span of time—is an organization of power—a variable combination of force and consent.

The Elements of National Power

I am aware, certainly, that the notion of power as exercised by states is more complex than the simple binomial of force and consent. More than sixty years ago, Hans Morgenthau identified the elements of national power as geography, natural resources, industrial capacity, military preparedness, population, national character, national morale, and the quality of diplomacy.[1] Recently Joseph Nye has advanced the notion of a nation's "soft power"—"getting others to want what you want"—in contrast to its "hard

---

1. Morgenthau, *Politics Among Nations*, 80–108.

power," that is, its military and economic capacity. He writes, "A country may obtain the outcomes it wants in world politics because other countries want to follow it, admiring its values, emulating its example, aspiring to its level of prosperity and openness."[2] Walter Russell Mead has extended the categories into what he calls sharp power (military), sticky power (economic), sweet power (American values and culture), and hegemonic power (the ability to set the agenda and frame the debate). The latter two are Mead's refinement of Nye's "soft power."[3] These distinctions support the analysis of power into its variable combination of force and consent.

The Concept of Relational Power

My own contribution to the analysis of power is to distinguish substantial power from relational power. Substantial power is the combination of elements of power a state actually has at its disposal and can bring to bear on the pursuit of foreign policy objectives—something like Morgenthau's enumeration of the elements of power plus Nye's soft power. Relational power is the ability of a state actually to use these elements of power to impose its will and/or achieve its objectives in particular situations. It is evident from even a cursory reading of contemporary international relations that the United States cannot do just anything it wants to do despite its massive military and other forms of power. Neither North Korea nor Iran is any match for the United States, militarily speaking, yet the U.S. has not been able to press either state to meet its demands and expectations. The hopes for making progress in that regard rest on the cooperation of other states—another form of relational power. The military might of the United States is designed to meet and defeat the forces of other states in large battles, but it adapts only with difficulty to "asymmetrical warfare"— the strategy of insurgents to turn their weakness into strength by employing tactics that make it difficult for the heavily armed, highly organized opponent to respond effectively. The use of improvised explosive devices (IEDs) and the retreat of insurgents into the shelter of civilian populations are cases in point. The prospects for success rely less on the preponderance of substantial power than on the ability actually to deploy it effectively in relation to the situation of conflict.

2. Nye, *Paradox of American Power*, 8–9.
3. Mead, *Power, Terror, Peace, and War*, 24–25.

WAR, PEACE, AND RECONCILIATION: PART TWO

Nuclear Weaponry as Relational Power

Let us apply the concept of relational power to the particular case of nuclear armaments. During the high-tension time of the nuclear standoff between the United States and the Soviet Union, it was said often that the two great powers had enough nuclear weapons and delivery systems to destroy the world's cities several times over. Why then the need for such excess destructive power? The question was of dubious relevance, because the intent of the weapons capability was not to destroy but to deter.[4] The operational question was the relational one: what kind and extent of nuclear systems capability does it take for each nation to constrain the military threats and actions of the other? In that setting, whoever engaged the morality of nuclear deterrence had to work through the ethical analysis of two issues, not just one. One issue was the moral usability of the weapons systems themselves—a problem dealt with by examining the weapons and their probable effects using just war *ius in bello* principles of discrimination and proportion. The question then was whether the utterly devastating effects of such weapons—ultimately affecting the entire world and incapable of making distinctions between combatants and noncombatants—would permit them to serve discriminately and proportionately any conceivable formulation of the just war *ius ad bellum* criterion of just cause. The answer, in brief, was no. The burden of proof here was on those who said nuclear weapons were justifiable, not on those who said they were not.

The other issue was what to do next, once one had decided that the weapons were inherently immoral and therefore morally unusable—but nevertheless existed and were central to the architecture of opposition between the superpowers. In this case the primary moral responsibility was not discharged by a judgment on the weapons systems, although that was part of the process of moral reasoning, but by designing a politics of carefully moving back from the brink while recognizing that the weaponry was a constant and inherent element of the political process. In other words, the inquiry into moral responsibility should start with the counterpoised

---

4. Note that I refer to the "high tension time" in Soviet-U.S. relationships, that is, to a point in the history of nuclear weapons development when both nations credibly could threaten each other with total destruction. Andrew Bacevich argues that when General Curtis LeMay was the head of Strategic Air Command, he built up a strike force with the purpose of destroying the Soviet Union totally, without regard to combatant-noncombatant distinctions or other moral limitations. The purpose was deterrence, but in LeMay's view no number of weapons and delivery systems was too high. Bacevich, *Washington Rules*, 43–57.

relationships of power and their implications, not with an abstract moral analysis of the weapons, and not even with a measurement of the elements of substantial power possessed by each side.

The dilemma posed by the juxtaposition of the two problems was that if one side began immediately to engage in nuclear disarmament (in consequence of deciding that the weapons were morally unusable), that move might dislodge the relational power system and bring about precisely the terrible destruction that the decision sought to avoid. That is, the opponent might see unilateral disarmament as a trick designed to draw it into an irreversible condition of vulnerability, or perhaps as evidence of weakness inviting attack. Moreover, elements of the political and military establishment of the disarming side very well might react negatively to the proposed change and use the occasion to seize power, thereby exacerbating the relational tensions. On the other hand, if the decision were taken gradually to defuse the situation by incremental means, the implication would be that nuclear deterrence is necessary to protect and assure the transition.[5] That implication would validate continued possession and positioning of the weapons systems, if only for that reason.

---

5. The original draft of Schema XIII of Vatican Council II included a flat rejection of the morality of nuclear deterrence. The final draft, in the "Constitution of the Church in the Modern World," Chapter V, Section 1, condemns total war and the indiscriminate destruction of cities and their populations but avoids a clear rejection of nuclear deterrence. Instead, it states vaguely that "many regard [nuclear deterrence] as the most effective way by which peace of a sort can be maintained between nations at the present time" (para. 81). It then goes on to warn about the insecurity and instability of the arms race. The United States Conference of Catholic Bishops, in their pastoral letter on war and peace ("The Challenge of Peace: God's Promise and Our Response," May 3, 1983), sustained the somber attitude toward nuclear war and deterrence, but built on a grudging concession by Pope John Paul II to declare, "Deterrence is not an adequate strategy as a long-term basis for peace; it is a transitional strategy justifiable only in conjunction with resolute determination to pursue arms control and disarmament" (from the Summary, Section I, B.3).

In 1986, the United Methodist bishops rejected nuclear deterrence but did not follow the logic of rejection to argue for immediate, unilateral disarmament. Instead, they advocated an "ethic of reciprocity" in which both sides would be encouraged to take incremental steps to avoid the ultimate terror. They did not face the obvious fact that reciprocity would work only if some degree of nuclear deterrence remained in place and the opposing sides continued to feel threatened by it. United Methodist Council of Bishops, *In Defense of Creation*, 47–48. For a spirited response to the bishops of his church, see Ramsey, *Speak Up for Just War or Pacifism*. My own contribution to the discussion can be found in *Modern War and the Pursuit of Peace*, reprinted in Thompson, *Moral Dimensions*, 283–314.

The point of this analysis is that nuclear weaponry must be understood and evaluated primarily as relational power in the context of the international system, not primarily as substantial and destructive force at the disposal of individual states. It is also the latter, of course, but the starting point for thinking about it is the counterpoised relationships of forces and the implications for everyone throughout the world of any disturbance of the anxious and fragile equilibrium. Moral questions must be raised about weapons as such, but the main context for moral and political analysis (they may come to the same thing) is the relational power system itself.

Nuclear Power and the International System

To pursue the truth of this claim, let us note that nuclear weaponry still plays an important role in the preoccupations of the international system and will continue to do so, but it is quite a different role from that of the years of the U.S.-Soviet rivalry. In those years the counterpoised nuclear weapons and their delivery mechanisms were central and integral to the architectural structure of the relationships that were most significant and most determinative in international society. Destabilization of that structure risked setting off the nuclear war that no one wanted. As we move along into the twenty-first century nuclear weapons and nuclear capabilities are a permanent and worrisome concern, but they do not dominate and threaten the international system to the extent and in the same ways that they did in the past. Which countries in the world must or can the United States deter relying primarily on nuclear power? None. To the extent that a policy of deterrence is necessary and relevant, the United States can implement it with nonnuclear power alone. North Korea and Iran are aspiring nuclear powers, but neither of them is a match for the U.S., militarily speaking, and they know it. The U.S. can destroy the military forces and the industrial capacity of either country without employing its nuclear armaments. China and the United States are respectful of each other's nuclear capabilities, but those capabilities are not central to the relationship as they were in the U.S.-Soviet opposition. At present, their competition mainly is economic. Deterrence doesn't work against terrorist activities, because terrorists have no state and no governmental structure to protect, and therefore cannot be deterred by threats of military reprisal of any kind. Moreover, they are suffused in a culture of martyrdom. They do not fear death; they welcome it.

However, to say that the United States does not need to deter with nuclear power is not to say that no other countries feel that way. Israel is not going to dismantle its (undisclosed) nuclear capabilities so long as Iran threatens it with destruction. India and Pakistan feel insecure vis-à-vis each other, and are not yet prepared to resolve the political differences that would allow them to get rid of that part of their weaponry and begin to work cooperatively on the solution of common problems. North Korea has decided—perhaps because of the example of Iraq—that it needs nuclear weapons in order to deter the United States. What this means is that there can be no elimination of nuclear weapons worldwide without the resolution of serious political differences and insecurities that lead some states to feel that the risk of having nuclear weapons is more tolerable than the risk of not having them. If all nuclear weapons were to be removed from everywhere, differences of interest would remain as would differentials of power. For that reason, nuclear disarmament cannot be approached as a problem in its own right apart from the organization of power in the international system.

Some of the systemic issues are clear and salient. If Iran develops a nuclear capability, for whatever reasons of its own, Saudi Arabia, Egypt, and Turkey may feel compelled to develop theirs also, thereby rearranging and destabilizing the balance of power in the Middle East. If North Korea succeeds in pursuing its nuclearizing mission, Japan and South Korea may consider it prudent to create their own nuclear capability. What, then, will be the responses of China and the United States? And then there are the problems of loose nukes, nuclear scientists for hire, nuclear entrepreneurs (e.g., the Pakistani A. Q. Khan), and the terrorist cells eager to get their hands on weapons of mass destruction that can be deployed without reliance on complicated and expensive delivery systems.

All of these problems are systemic within the international organization of power. They are not problems of nuclear weapons only or even exclusively of individual states. Nuclear weapons to one degree or another will continue to be an element in whatever organization of power constitutes world peace in the present and future, as well as a threatening element of instability in the organization. To control their production, proliferation, and possible deployment is a task not for the International Atomic Energy Agency alone or the United Nations or individual interested states, nor is it a task discharged by a policy of nuclear disarmament. It is a problem of full international cooperation—a matter of the organization of power in the comprehensive international system. What is essential is that nuclear weapons systems not be allowed to organize the peace around their own potential for destruction, but that they be constrained and limited within the relational system of force and consent organized by the international system as a whole.

The Analysis and Its Prospects

This descriptive and analytical approach tells us that power is not inherently contradictory either to reconciliation or to peace. The reduction of the theoretical contradiction requires the advancement of consent over force in the practical exercise and organization of power. It requires also a determined process of the civilization of power to equip consent with the institutional means of giving it authority and stability. The civilization process will provide different possibilities for peace as an organization of power, and thereby for improved efficacy for reconciliation in relation to war. We shall turn now to an examination of this process.

8

The Civilizing of Power

The movement from war to politics, or the politics of peace in the ending of war, is a process of the civilizing of power. It is a civilizing process, that is, when it is seriously political, and not merely peace as a continuing, unilateral imposition of force by the victor. By the "civilizing of power" I mean moving the results of war from primary reliance on force to greater reliance on consent—a fundamental change in the reality of peace as the organization of power. It is the process of institutionalizing power relations, overcoming their random movements and unpredictability, removing some degree of substantial power from the exclusive control of competing entities, making power more an instrument of emergent community, subordinating some behaviors to law, and conferring greater authority on the exercise of power. By "seriously political," I mean much the same, with the addition and emphasis of political will to make such things happen. It is the will to accept the self-limiting discipline of contracts, laws, and customs, in place of unilateral efforts to translate substantial power into relational power.

In the history of political thought this process sometimes is referred to as politicization—domesticating power in a *polis* (to use the Aristotelian concept)—or as socialization (in the sociological, not the Marxist, sense), symbolized in various situations as the formation of competing forces into a *civitas*, or a *societas*. The symbol of the *polis*, or "perfect society," used widely in Thomistic political thought, proposes a more integrated degree and articulated form of political society than international relations are likely to achieve; nevertheless, it points to prospects for ordering, coherence, and authority that may help guide emergent negotiations over how to live together without fighting, and even how to cooperate in the support of common goals and interests. The same may be said, perhaps somewhat less than more (with different linguistic and cultural meanings), of the symbol of the *civitas*. *Societas* symbolizes linkage and the presence of elements of common culture and consciousness. It implies less political integration than the other two, but for that reason may be more reflective of the process of civilization of power in the international system.

A clarification: the term *civilization*, as used here, refers to the process of creating political and legal linkages among entities that have been at war, thereby allowing and requiring them to deal with each other in ways that govern their intercourse without hostility and resort to violence. This usage carries no implication of imposing one particular civilization on another, no supposition that some parties to the process are culturally superior to other parties. It is not to be confused with imperial civilizing efforts such as Alexander the Great's spreading of Hellenistic culture, Kipling's British mission to "lesser breeds without the law," the extension of the territory of Islam to impose *Shari'a* law, or global salvation via the spreading of a free enterprise economic system. It is a process of institutionalizing power, not of cultural conversion, even though cultural values assuredly will come into play as individual parties negotiate the construction of a new organization of power. However, the process may require bringing some states, perceived as troublemakers, into an existing system with the expectation that they will adhere to the system's established rules, laws, and practices. Perhaps that established system may be termed a "civilization," in some sense, but the civilizing process in such cases intends to impart a culture only in the sense of norms that support international cooperation and suppress or deflect inclinations to make war or otherwise destabilize the international system.

Aspects of the Civilization of Power

The inclusive pattern of activity in the civilization of power is from politics to war to politics. War is a disruption of the political order. The movement from war to politics is to restore order of some kind in patterns of relationship that suppress the resort to arms and violence in favor of regulated approaches to the resolution of differences. One names these patterns "peace," in the normative sense intended here, when the resulting historical reality is common agreement to exist and proceed, and not the imposition of force by one side on the other. Insofar as the peace intended is the freedom to be vulnerable, the process toward that end is the civilization of power.

THE CIVILIZING OF POWER

Let us consider some of the aspects of the process of civilization.

1. As I have said, the civilizing of power is the movement from force to consent as the predominating form of power in the organization of relationships. In an earlier analysis I defined power as a variable combination of force and consent. In actual history, the combination can be dramatically one-sided. Force may predominate, with only a minimal element of consent. Or consent may be the primary constituent of communal power, with force present only as a modest degree of policing. Or there may be mediating situations where society is either disintegrating and inviting more forcible resolution, or increasing its coherence through reduction of dependence on forcible control. In the latter case, that is, in the movement from predominance of force to predominance of consent in the organization of societal cohesion, one observes what I call the civilization of power. Power becomes processively more *civil*, in that it is increasingly generated out of consent and obligated to the consenters, and less a matter of the imposition of naked force.

2. The notion of civilization, in this usage, is a process of creating community. As noted above, ancient philosophers used the terms *civitas* and *societas* to symbolize the greater or lesser degrees of societal and relational integration. The community, civilized thusly, is neither radically individualistic nor absolute in unification. The social reality is not that of a single individual or a small group dominating a mass of subjects, nor is it a swarm of disconnected individuals grasping for means to express and protect themselves. It is an organic integration of persons who identify themselves with reference to the community-coming-into-being but without losing their sense of personal identity. To use a popular expression, they are persons-in-community. The persons in the web of social relationships find their identity in and through these relationships, and without these relationships would have a different identity—or perhaps none at all. Nevertheless, they remain individuated, and do not simply submerge their identities in a fully integrated social whole.

3. The movement from force to consent as the primary principle of social organization, accompanied by the growing integration toward community, is expressed also in the redistribution of authority. This process is a movement toward the effectuation of membership, toward

participation in benefits, opportunities, and obligations by all members at every level. The civilization of power breaks down the restrictive barriers of caste, race, religion, and privilege to draw all persons in the society into full membership. Therefore it implies the diffusion of authority throughout the body politic, the authorization of command and control over the whole group by all of the members. One might refer to this as the "democratization of power," if one means by that the ownership of public institutions and processes by all the members and not simply the holding of elections to choose representatives and leaders. It is the creation of an integrated community, to the degree that consent becomes predominant over force in the process. The institutions of law, leadership, and organization do not disappear into direct action by the masses. They remain as instruments of decision and protection, but those who operate the institutions are not a law unto themselves. They are responsible to those who broadly give their consent to governing.

4. Likewise, neither the police force nor the military establishment of the community is disbanded. They remain as instruments of the community for pursuing its needs and interests, both domestically and internationally. But both police and military power are subordinate to civilian control. They do not have independent presence or authority to decide what those needs and interests are and to drag the rest of the community behind them in their efforts to control them. This development is an essential consequence of the civilization of power, of the movement from force to consent as the organizing principle of the society.

Globalization and Its "Rule Sets"

Several proposals for the civilization of power in international relations have been set forth. One is offered by Thomas P. M. Barnett. As reported previously, in *The Pentagon's New Map* Barnett criticizes the Pentagon for thinking of war only in the context of war, instead of in the context of *everything else*.[1] He means "everything else" quite literally, because war connects and affects well beyond the relatively limited concern with military issues, whether tactical or strategic. More specifically, however, he means that

1. Barnett, *The Pentagon's New Map*.

war should be examined and interpreted in the context of globalization. In putting the matter this way he intends to shift the context of war from the primacy of interstate relations to the large and expanding economic currents that often create the opportunities and necessities for the behavior of states in international politics. His "new map" displays the patterns of integrating and non-integrating states, that is, those states that participate significantly in globalization and those that do not. In his view, these distinctions are basic to the dynamics of international politics, and therefore to the prospects for war. States that are integrated into globalization are less likely to make war with each other, because they accept the new rule sets that globalization requires and provides. States not thusly integrated do not accept the rule sets unless forced to do so. That is, they are likely to attract war and to make war. Barnett writes,

> In the era of globalization, we draw [the] line between those parts of the world that are actively integrating their national economies into a global economy, or what I call globalization's Functioning Core, and those that are failing to integrate themselves into that larger economic community and all the rule sets it generates, or those states I identify as constituting the Non-Integrating Gap. Simply put, when we see countries moving toward the acceptance of globalization's economic rule sets, we should expect to see commensurate acceptance of an emerging global security rule set—in effect, agreement on why, and under what conditions, war makes sense.[2]

These patterns are the main elements of the "everything else" in the context of which war must be understood.

In this vision of international reality, the threats to peace arise from the disconnectedness among non-integrating states and between those states and the integrating states. "Eradicating disconnectedness, therefore, becomes the defining security task of our age."[3] Peace is promoted by bringing non-integrating states into the process of globalization with the understanding that they accept the rule sets that enable the process: "Rather than dwell on the unpredictability of future threats or attacks, our strategic vision for national security needs to focus on growing the community of states that recognize a stable set of rules."[4] States and other groups that

2. Ibid., 25–26.
3. Ibid., 8.
4. Ibid., 25.

reject connectedness and promote chaos invite forcible restraint. That is one of the moral and political bases for resisting and attacking terrorists, as well as rogue states and failed or failing states that threaten the security of the system. Terrorism in particular is dedicated to promoting disconnectedness in the international system and thwarting prospects for integration.

Barnett does not refer to this proposal as the civilizing of power, although that is what he is describing and proposing. Independent, unpredictable, irrational power comes under a system of control defined by the rule sets of globalization. There is nothing in the process to suggest that one particular civilization—for example, Western liberal internationalism, or Islam in some form—makes peace by drawing everyone else into its own cultural rule sets. This "civilization" has a prudential basis: states buy into it because doing so serves their own security and economic interests. When arbitrary power enters into a system of control, that is, when it becomes socialized and loses some degree of independence, it participates in a process of civilization.

This process operates by consent, the increase of which is the mark of the civilizing of power. "Likewise, wherever rules are clear because most players in that system agree they're good, there's not as much enforcement required, because most participants simply decide on their own that playing by the rules is the best course of action."[5] States consent to the rules because they believe it is in their interest to do so. They want to share in the benefits of globalization, and they want the security that results when all other states observe the rule sets. Of course, we are not talking about pure consent. Some states must be "encouraged" to join the club and accept the rules, and all of them know that there are penalties for violating the rules. But the civilization of power requires only a movement toward greater consent, not a final condition where force or threat of force is absent. Nor are we talking about consent in electoral terms. The issue for the civilizing of power is that those who come under the requirements of an organization of power submit to them by agreement, not because the requirements are imposed by force.

The Postmodern State: Prospects and Alternatives

A different kind of proposal for the international system is put forward by Robert Cooper in *The Breaking of Nations: Order and Chaos in the*

5. Ibid., 22.

Twenty-First Century.[6] Cooper acknowledges the process of globalization and its implications but does not make it central to his analysis and recommendations. Instead, he focuses on two main points concerning international society, its tendencies, and its needs. The first is that what hitherto has been the central theater of international interaction—namely, Europe and the Atlantic Community—has emerged from a condition in which the main controls on violence were the balance of power, which may include alliances, and hegemony or empire. These options do not work anymore. Balance of power essentially is a defensive option based on the suspicion that opponents are likely to attack and must be resisted, if not by unilateral efforts then by combinations of opposing states' power. In this former "central theater" the balance of power is not needed anymore, for the primary reason that the states do not want to fight each other, and knowing this about each other, they do not fear attack. Technological advances, especially the advent of nuclear weapons, have encouraged this development, as have the memories of the devastation of past wars, and lately the fear of chaos deriving from threats of terrorism and threats from failed and rogue states elsewhere. And none of the participating states itches for empire any longer, because acquiring additional territory tends to be unprofitable, and because governing unwilling subjects is such a demanding chore. These states, then, are fashioning new modes of relationship, with new forms of subordinating the phenomenon of violence.

This development is of special significance for both the theory and practice of international politics. Heretofore it has been assumed, especially in realist political theory, that balance of power, hegemony, and empire are permanent and universalizable strategies—or at least tendencies—in relationships among states. What the European development shows is that they are particular to historical conditions and may not be relevant prescriptions for other times and circumstances. It shows also, and in consequence, that relationships among states are not inevitably and everywhere expressed in competition over power and interest.

Cooper's second main point is that international society is neither a disconnected array of sovereign states nor a single, unified order, but a collection of three types of society, each with a characteristic relationship to the institution of the state and each with corresponding tendencies for dealing with violence and chaos. What he calls the *modern* pattern is the familiar national state system alluded to above, with its stress on sovereignty,

6. Cooper, *The Breaking of Nations.*

monopoly of violence, and secrecy concerning its military capabilities. Its means of dealing with violence and chaos beyond its control are the devices previously discussed: balance of power, alliances, hegemony, empire. The *premodern* pattern displays a state that is relatively weak in relation to internal social forces. Society is chaotic, with nongovernmental forces attempting to exert control and extend it in relation to governmental institutions for which they have little use or respect. Violence clearly is not a monopoly of the state. It may be individualized, or controlled by segments of society contending against the government and each other. At present, such societies may remain isolated because larger countries no longer want to build empires, but their potential for exporting chaos may become the occasion for what Cooper calls "defensive imperialism," that is, intervention in "premodern" societies to forestall the spread of disintegration elsewhere.

The third pattern is the *postmodern* state. In his view it represents the collapse of the "modern" state system upwards into a realm of inter-state associations that serve common needs and assume intrusive powers but fall short of becoming international governments. States do not disappear in this pattern, but they become much less self-protective and controlling. As indicated above, they do not fear attack from their neighbors. Therefore they do not prepare for war against them. They devalue the importance of national sovereignty, accept a large degree of intrusiveness into their internal life, and open their military establishments to inspection by other states and international agencies. *Postmodern* is a condition of vulnerability that depends on the building of trust and the turning of enmity into friendship, but without surrendering national identity and some degrees of state control. This is the pattern that has emerged in Europe, after centuries of suspicion, secrecy, defensiveness, enmity, and warfare.

One is justified in concluding that for Robert Cooper *postmodern* is the normative pattern for states. It is the condition toward which all states should move in order to promote peace that is both durable and just. Nevertheless, he does not argue that all states in fact are moving that way, or that they are likely to do so, or necessarily do behave that way even if they have achieved the status of postmodernity. All three patterns are present in the contemporary world at the same time. Most of the really big states—China, India, the United States—fall into the modern category, even though they do exhibit some tendencies toward postmodernity. They guard their sovereignty and prefer the security they provide for themselves to the security of transnational relationships accompanied by openness, transparency, and vulnerability. "Modern" states can dissolve and revert to conditions of premodernity, losing their monopoly of violence and their control of large areas of public life. Even postmodern states may behave like modern states, throwing aside the rules of postmodernity and fighting wars when modern states provoke them to do so, or when they feel that their existence is threatened. And furthermore, and not simply incidentally, the postmodern system works only because, according to Cooper, it is guaranteed by the military power of the United States.

However, the postmodern pattern remains the best hope for controlling violence and thereby organizing and preserving peace, especially in view of technological development and the continuing threats of chaos. Other states outside the European orbit are moving in that direction. It is a tenuous and uncertain prospect, but one to be guided and nurtured. However, the postmodern ambitions cannot avoid the fact that control of violence is a complex process in an international system composed of all three types of states. Depending on times, places, and circumstances, several methods will be pertinent to the civilizing of power: international associations, defensive imperialism, balance of power, unilateral national efforts, and postmodern cooperation and vulnerability.

"The National Security Strategy" and the Civilizing of Power

The United States, as indicated, is placed by Cooper in the category of modern state, not postmodern, and certainly not premodern. It is preoccupied by pursuit of its own interests and resists transparency and loss of secrecy. The United States is involved heavily in creating international institutions and participating in them, and these are postmodern tendencies, but usually it exercises a large amount of influence in such institutions, and it rejects surrendering its sovereignty to them. A major example of the latter is its refusal to come under the jurisdiction of the International Court of Justice.

This designation as a "modern state," together with its qualifications, comes to expression in "The National Security Strategy of the United States of America," published on September 17, 2002.[7] The intent of that document is not to discuss the civilization of power as such, but to do as the title indicates—propose a security strategy for the United States. The problem

7. I offered a critical evaluation of the document in "Power Play: The New 'National Security Strategy.'"

to be managed is not that of arranging the organization of power for peace with particular enemies, but of dealing with a global mix of conflict and cooperation. Difficulties for this organization are created in the first instance by terrorism equipped with modern technology, but also by continuing friction among great powers, localized conflict with wider disruptive implications, and the prospect of regional powers rising to threaten the security of the United States. If one can speak of the "civilizing" of a power system to deal with these difficulties, it is a process of maintaining cooperative relationships among the "great powers," building international institutions to deal effectively with various relational problems and local conflicts, forming "coalitions of the willing" to deal with particular issues beyond the reach or competence of international institutions, and shaping a "balance of power for freedom." The most ambitious aspect of the proposal is in effect a transformation of the world to establish societies everywhere on the principles of liberty, democracy, and free markets. Supporting the entire project is the military and economic power of the United States, maintained and exercised not only to secure the interests of the United States but also to discharge for the world as a whole the responsibilities of dominant power.[8]

The last two provisions in particular make clear that, despite its global reach and declaration of global responsibility, the strategy issues from what Cooper defines as a modern, not a postmodern, state. There is no surrender of sovereignty, or even a serious modification of it. American national interests are paramount, even if modified in places by international interests and the interests of other nations. The U.S. reserves to itself the right to act unilaterally and even to engage in preemptive (properly termed "preventive," in some instances) actions when its interests so require. "Coalitions of the willing" are *ad hoc* combinations of allies to pursue international objectives of the United States when international institutions are not supportive or relevant. Presumably these coalitions will shape and maintain the "balances of power for freedom," not otherwise defined, and clearly

---

8. See Project for a New American Century, "Rebuilding America's Defenses." This report is much more direct and aggressive in affirming America's military, economic, and technological superiority and dominance in the world. It calls for a grand strategy with enhanced military capability to maintain and extend American control of world situations and events. The germ of the report was in a directive from the Defense Department under then Secretary of Defense Richard Cheney. Several of the signers later became members of the Bush administration. One may speculate that "Rebuilding America's Defenses" provides the underlying intent of National Security Strategy 2002. If so, that would point to an important difference between declaratory policy and actual policy in Bush's neoconservative foreign policy.

not balances of the traditional type—which would come into existence, in some instances, to balance the power of the United States. This proposal for "civilizing" global power issues from the national capital of the one superpower; it is not a process of common discipline and exchange worked out—as in the case of Europe—by states attempting to shape a common, benign future against the background of a hostile and destructive past. Moreover, the proposed transformation of societies the world over to the principles of liberty, democracy, and capitalism reads less like a neutral process of taming and organizing power than a missionary capturing of ideologically and religiously diverse societies by a historically developed civilization with what seems to many—but certainly not all—to be a really good set of ideas.

Of course, there are numerous practical problems that I cannot discuss here: democracy requires institution building and other societal conditions, not simply free elections; free elections and other liberties are a necessary part of the mix, but are resisted by autocratic states that are important allies of the United States; not all societies see free markets and capitalism as the way to secular salvation; American society is conflicted over how much and what kind of capitalism it wants; and human rights advocacy encounters sharp opposition from some aspects of Islamic religion and culture. And there are dilemmas: if this grand vision succeeds, the United States will have to relocate itself within the new organization of power—in a subordinate role, honoring the liberty, democracy, and maturity of other participating states. In effect, it will work itself out of its job, or at least out of its role as the dominant power. If that seems like a good thing, which in most respects it is, the outcome exposes another dilemma: Cooper argues that the postmodern pattern extended to the world probably will not work unless the power of the United States continues to guarantee it. The United States seems fated to remain primarily a modern state in the larger process of civilizing international power into postmodernity, limited by aspects of a world that does not allow the full translation of its substantial power into effective relational power.

In the contemporary world the civilizing of power requires both a constancy of concept and a change of focus. It is about organizing peace into a more coherent association, about moving from greater force to greater consent, institutionalizing the means of power, creating a firmer and deepening web of relationships, disciplining war in the context of everything else. That is the conceptual dimension. The focus moves, however. In the traditional process from politics to war to politics, the focus is on particular states in conflict with each other. Now it is on the international system as the connector of states and therefore as the structural means of overcoming and controlling violence. The program for civilizing power requires the incremental development of layers of social connectedness that states allow to control aspects of their behavior, and do so because they find this limited control beneficial—not only to serve particular interests but also because they affirm a social mechanism for making the world more orderly. Their commitment, therefore, is to accept particular limitations and directives by entering the system, and also to join in protecting the system itself. I have sketched several proposals for recognizing and facilitating a connective international system. They differ in important respects, but they agree in recognizing both that a connecting process is underway and that it is the mechanism for dealing with the control of violence.

There are limits to this process. One is that it does not do away with the state system as such. It cannot overcome the mixture of postmodern, modern, and premodern states in the system—to use Cooper's typology. In this continuing mix the collective civilizing of power internationally imposes some limits on sovereignty but does not eliminate important elements of state control. It dissuades uses of military force and provides alternatives for the pursuit of interests and the addressing of grievances, but it does not categorically exclude war for just cause and as last resort. However, it does diversify authorization for the use of military power. States will continue to authorize their own uses of force when they are threatened directly and seriously, but for other occasions where military force may seem appropriate they will need to seek international authorization of some kind and degree.

A second limit is that the civilizing of power is never-ending. There is no final state of civilization that establishes an enduring benign international order, permanently controlling violence and guaranteeing peace. Whatever form of connection may be established is a product of history, constantly shifting, threatened from within and without, with no "end of history." The politics of peace is a continuing process. The reordering of power requires tending and constant vigilance.

9
The International System, and Other Matters

The international system is the matrix within which to contemplate the movement from war to peace through the civilization of power. It is the fundamental framework for political theorizing, for analyzing concepts of interest, for discerning responsibilities, permissions, and limits in the exercising of power, and for exploring questions of authorization. It is the total web of connections among whatever constitutes the *everything else* that Thomas Barnett distinguishes from war itself. The system is the particular historical order of which war at any given time is an institution. One must examine the nature and meaning of this concept in order to understand basic aspects of the civilization of power and how that understanding relates to the analysis of war in the context of politics.

Many years ago, when I used the term in a presentation to a conference on ethics and international politics, an international relations scholar of some eminence declared to the audience and to me that there was no such thing as an "international system." That comment struck me as odd, because quite obviously there were and are systems of relationships among states and other entities in the international realm, and many of these had and have duration and some efficacy relative to their purposes. Also, the term was used widely and routinely in the literature of international politics. All I could imagine that he meant was that there was no world government, nothing organized from the top that provided regulation, order, and control, nothing that could actively and authoritatively "systematize" the chaos. That was true, of course, and still is, but the admission does not add up to a conclusion that there is no international system, in the sense of systemic relationships among interacting parties in international society. The patterns of relationships change form and membership, but they constitute nonetheless a system of connections within the larger political world.

The International System and the State System

Often the international system is equated with the state system. Historically that equation has made sense, for at least two reasons. One is that an active and identifiable system came into existence only with the emergence of the nation-state following the breakup of Christendom and the medieval empire. The other is that the states in fact create and are actors in a system of relationships—one that both affects military conflict (among other matters) and is affected by it, and is the primary system to which the world as a whole must pay heed. In the traditional realist paradigm this system is the pattern of interaction among states, mainly states of some significant power, and more particularly European states—and eventually, and quite prominently, the United States of America. Essentially it has been a system of power relations, not organized from the top, not contained and directed by an inclusive and authorizing international institution, but managed by alliances, balances, hegemonies, treaties, enduring wariness and manipulations, and threats and occasional outbreaks of violent conflict.

Now the system is worldwide, and by no means exclusively European. Henry Kissinger has argued that in fact there now are four international systems: the United States and Western Europe, the great powers of Asia (India, China, Japan, Russia), the Middle East, and the African continent.[1] This listing intends only to call attention to the great diversity of systems and their worldwide spread compared to the old European state system, and does not mean to exclude the more comprehensive system of relationships among and within these four groupings and between and among individual states, as well as nonstatal elements. In addition to the relatively strong and stable states, the international system includes "rogue" states, failed or failing states, self-isolating states, nonnuclear states with nuclear ambitions, states harboring terrorist leaders and movements—any organizations or disorganizations of power that might threaten the relative stability of the system itself.[2] It includes also international institutions of various kinds and

1. Kissinger, *Does American Need a Foreign Policy?*, 25–26.
2. See the aforementioned work by Robert Cooper, *The Breaking of Nations*, in which he categorizes components of the international system as premodern states, modern states, and postmodern states.

scope, international law, patterns of customary behavior, multifarious economic organizations and tendencies, and humanitarian nongovernmental organizations.

Is it defensible any longer to speak of the international system as a *state* system? As we have seen, the diversity of composition goes well beyond an association of states alone. True enough, the current international system clearly is much more complex and comprehensive than the state system of the realist paradigm. Nevertheless, at its operative center it remains a state system. International laws and organizations may develop organically to the point where they have some controlling efficacy that the individual states must heed, but they are creatures of the states, much of their authority derives from them, and often what they demand is frustrated or even vetoed by states when individual states judge that international efforts run contrary to their interests. These organic inter-state or supra-state institutions must operate together with the states as aspects of the international system, and not as autonomous systems.

Moreover, does the state continue to be the predominating institution in the system? I am aware, certainly, of the objection that the national state, which arose in the course of Western history, is passing from the scene as an effective historical actor. My response, paraphrasing Mark Twain, is that reports of its demise are quite premature. The point in regard to the obsolescence of the national state often is made with reference to globalization, that is, to the emergence of transnational economic forces that find national boundaries and state authority to be a nuisance and develop skills in ignoring or overriding them. That argument indeed is strong, but it is less compelling since the severe economic recession of late 2008 and following weakened some of these international economic forces and threw control back to the states. The states were and are the power centers that had to fund and administer stimulus packages, bail out international financial institutions, and begin the process of reregulating autonomous economic powers. Moreover, as Robert Kagan has argued, the rise of globalization actually has enhanced the power of particular states and encouraged their expansionist tendencies.[3]

More permanently and integrally to their functions in the international system, states are the institutions that control the weapons systems, which they increase or diminish in relation to their perceptions of interest and security. In particular, states are the institutions that develop and

3. Kagan, *The Return of History and the End of Dreams*.

control nuclear weapons and their delivery systems, and they work strenuously to keep them out of the hands of terrorists, other nonstatal actors, and weak or rogue states. It is true, of course, that the international system is no longer essentially a *military power* system, by contrast with the assumptions of the realist paradigm. Barnett's focus on the prominence if not predominance of globalization points to patterns of association and relationship not reducible to military capabilities and expectations. Also, one should be ever mindful of Joseph Nye's insistence on the importance of what he calls "soft power." Nevertheless, military capabilities—present and potential—remain a fundamental element of the power held and disposed of in and throughout the international system. Witness the anxiety and effort focused on nuclear proliferation, and the unease over whether some states are building up their military forces, and for what purposes. To quote Francis Fukuyama, "What only states and states alone are able to do is aggregate and purposefully deploy legitimate power. This power is necessary to enforce a rule of law domestically, and it is necessary to preserve world order internationally. Those who have argued for a 'twilight of sovereignty'—whether they are proponents of free markets on the right or committed unilateralists on the left—have to explain what will replace the power of sovereign nation-states in the contemporary world."[4]

The international system is neither an ideal construct nor a permanent artifact. It changes form, scope, and membership with the multifarious shifts in human history. What does remain constant is its foundation in the inter-state system, whatever differences in composition and configuration the system of interacting states may take. The point here is not to give a full description and analysis of the international system but to disclose the range of vision within which war must be discerned and understood. War affects not only the immediate adversaries but the system as a whole. States and other entities not immediate parties to the conflict may see their interests affected by threats of systemic shock and dislocation. They may look for ways to intervene, directly or indirectly. What is necessary now is to identify and analyze some of the principal ways in which the perspective from within the international system affects the understanding of the responsibilities and dispositions of power.

---

4. Fukuyama, *State-Building*, 120. See also Kagan, *The Return of History*: "The world has not been transformed. In most places, the nation-state remains as strong as ever, and so, too, the nationalist ambitions, the passions, and the competition among nations that have shaped history" (3).

System Thinking and Political Theorizing

The traditional way to think theoretically about international politics is to begin with the state and project outwards. Political theory is theory of the state. Whatever the state encounters and must contend with in its external relations is explained and dealt with in the context of the state's self-understanding and interests. The point is expressed in the fact that *reason of state* became the ultimate criterion of judgment in international relations with the emergence of the state system. However, when international politics expanded to global inclusiveness, and the concept of an international system began to claim influence and indeed primacy in that inclusiveness, the process of theorizing had to take account of changes in its sources. It is not possible to dismiss the role of the state, but neither is it acceptable to derive the theory of international politics exclusively from the state and its interests. Now the international system becomes the primary context for theorizing, and the role of the states is redefined within that system. The result is that all or almost all of the aspects of international relations must be rethought to take account of this refocusing. Such rethinking pertains to the concepts of interest and responsibility, to authorization for the uses of power, to the meaning and application of just war criteria, and to the care of the international system itself—among other matters.

On the other hand, there has been no simple switch from one source of theorizing to the other. As I have argued, the state system is the basis of and fundamental operative mechanism (so to speak) within the international system. The persistence of state responsibility and the reality of state power continue to motivate and shape statal ways of thinking and acting. Expectations generated from within the workings of the international system interact with the inclinations of the states. Increasingly, the former may influence and even compel the latter, but they do not simply replace them. The continuing reality is a duality of definitions and claims. This clashing duality is the subject matter of foreign policy, and often the determinant of the resort to and conduct of war.

Redefining "Interest"

The first question of justification for any move in foreign policy, especially one involving the use of military force, is whether it is in support of a national interest. The presumption is that the government goes ahead with the move if it does represent an interest—in particular a so-called vital interest—and if resources and other relevant factors support it. The government does not pursue the matter if it is not a serious interest, whatever its resources may be. The criterion is ambiguous in that defining the interest may be a limiting factor—ruling out actions that are not in the national interest—or an expansive factor, reaching out to ambitions that heretofore have not been part of the definition of national interest (that is, a defense of aggressive and acquisitive behavior). But the policy moves in either case toward what the government decides is the national interest and how the nation's power should pursue it.

When the context of the international system is introduced, the concept of interest becomes much more complex, even from the standpoint of the individual state acting in international politics. The state then no longer is able to ask in simplistic and straightforward terms what is and is not in its interest. The shape, membership, condition, and future of the international system all are matters of national interest. Accordingly, a state must ask how developments in the system of relationships affect its defensive and projective uses of power. In March 2011, the United States involved itself directly in NATO actions against the forces of Colonel Muammar Ghadafi, which were attempting to restore him to absolute power in Libya by destroying the popular elements rising against him. American critics of the U.S. involvement argued that it should not participate, because doing so did not support any U.S. national interest. Of course, they were using "interest" in the previously established sense: neither the U.S. nor any ally had been attacked by Libya, the U.S. had no territorial presence or claims there, it was not dependent on Libya for oil, etc. However, that nation's—and other nations'—interests had been redefined by the entanglement of the Libyan events in the international system. The United States had an interest in the impact of events in Libya on other happenings in the roiling Middle East; in the relevance of NATO to a serious political dislocation in its neighborhood; in the implications of a collapsed North African and Arabic country for the expansion of terrorist movements, especially Al-Qaeda; and in the prospect of whether the Security Council of the United Nations would provide a legal basis for dealing with the protection of threatened Libyan civilians. All of these "interest" issues were generated by the entwining of the Libyan problem with the international system. That being so, it was possible no longer to act solely on a traditional concept of national interest. On the other hand, neither is it possible simply to dismiss the traditional concept. There well may be occasions when a stricter concept of national interest must be applied to justify, reject, or limit uses of national power—perhaps when system-defined interests are not present, or perhaps even when they are. The duality of national-international continues.

Moreover, there are and increasingly will be problems of the international system as such, which may or may not be of direct or immediate relevance to historic interests of particular states. They are system-generated interests, which may come into view for states when they touch them directly, but nevertheless are of continuing interest to them precisely because the states are integrated into the system in which the problems occur and have a spreading impact.

International terrorist movements present a problem of that kind, as do "rogue" states, and also nuclear weapons possession and proliferation. The role of oil, its locations and transportation through pipelines and open sea lanes, is an international systemic issue, and not only a concern of individual states. Robert Cooper has written of the possibility of a "defensive imperialism," by which he means that established powers may have to move into collapsed societies ("premodern states") in order to prevent their infecting the international system with their dysfunctional implications.[5]

The point of this exploration is to show that the international system makes a difference in how we conceptualize interest. National interest must be redefined with respect to its engagement with international systemic realities. Problems within the international system must be discerned as matters that require both international cooperation and—at times—the direct attention of particular states. If the system in its present organic and relational character cannot disconnect from the state system, neither can the state system ignore or defy the inclusiveness and expectations of the international system. The instrument and occasions of war cannot avoid being influenced by this system-driven reconceptualization of the meaning of interest.

Authority and Military Power

In the just war ethic, one of the criteria for justifying resort to war is *competent authority*, referred to also as legitimate authority. In one respect it is a matter of deciding who has the right to commit the state to war, in another of deciding whether an exercise of military power should be

---

5. Cooper, *Breaking of Nations*, 18.

allowed. The latter respect is the important one, once the states control and dispose of military power. Under the old system of *Realpolitik* a state felt sufficiently authorized to use war as an instrument of national policy if the usage served some national interest, especially what was considered a vital interest. The rulers decided the case and did not have to get clearance from the pope, their people, or anyone else. With the shift from absolutist rule to democratic participation, the support of the people became an important if not essential condition. Consent to military action might be given institutionally through the people's representatives in Parliament or Congress, or it might be present informally but effectively in the government's sense of whether the population will support a particular military action made purportedly in their name. By either means the will of the people is the condition of authorization.

With the emergence of the international system as an inclusive context for world politics and other matters, that system itself becomes the larger context for authorization of uses of force to pursue state objectives. It is by no means the sole referee of authorization, and often not the most important one, but its presence and claims cannot be ignored. The international system does not simply override the authority of governments and their respective peoples, but it does create expectations that governments will respect international norms and will not use military force as an instrument of policy merely because they want to do so and believe they can get away with it. The concept of national interest has not been set aside. But the principle of reason of state no longer suffices as the criterion of military action. There are international laws and covenants governing resort to war. States like to claim—and to believe—that they are conforming to these international permissions and limits when they use military force. Moreover, governments find it important in most cases to seek support for a proposed action from a resolution of the United Nations Security Council.

One could see this quest for international system authorization in operation in 2003, when the United States pressed hard for a resolution from the United Nations Security Council to support its plan to attack Saddam Hussein and his forces in Iraq. When the resolution was not forthcoming, the United States attacked anyway, claiming a kind of international authorization from what the Bush administration termed a "coalition of the willing." It was clear at the time that the United States had no real need for the increments to military power provided by members of the coalition. It had overwhelming force in place already, and was going to do whatever it intended to do, but it placed some value on this means of authorization. The primary purpose of the "coalition" was to give a covering of international authority to a unilateral action.

Also, the Bush administration claimed justification for unilateral action on the grounds that its military action was a preemptive attack.[6] A preemptive attack is a defensive move to block an assault on the homeland or its forces that purportedly is about to take place. The United Nations Charter allows for such demonstrably defensive actions, a provision that provides authorization from the international system. In that particular case, however, there was no evidence of an imminent attack by Iraq on the United States. The purpose of the action by the United States military was to destroy the real or prospective capability of Iraq to make such an attack in the future. That is what is known as *preventive* war, not *preemptive* war. Preventive war is not sanctioned by the U.N. Charter. One might make a case for it, but only when there is wide international support. In that case, the action no longer is unilateral, or one justified simply by reason of state, but one that claims and is limited by authorization conferred by the international system.[7]

Undoubtedly there are and will be occasions when a state will engage in military action that has no overt international sanction of any kind but that the state believes to be reasonable and necessary. It may perceive vagueness or a gap in legal provisions, or may simply decide that the weight of interest in the particular case is sufficient to allow it to ignore a law, or custom, or resolution, or deliberately violate it. On such occasions, which one hopes will be exceedingly rare, any state that has any pretensions to regard and support the international system should apply this principle: Attempt to act in such manner as to draw consent from other states for what it is doing illegally or outside the law. In a sense it is asking whether other states probably would do the same thing in the same situation. Obviously, that is a highly subjective criterion, and clearly open to self-serving interpretation and rationalization. Nevertheless, it reflects awareness of the international system and of the need for authorization beyond what is given by a state's interests and its own popular support. By using this principle,

   6. See "The National Security Strategy of the United States, September 2002," III, 6. The precise reference here is to the "war against terrorists," but the Bush administration later interpreted the fight with Iraq as the main battleground of that war, and indeed used this justification of preemptive war to cover what in fact was a preventive attack.
   7. For my comments on the use of "preemptive attack" when what really is meant is "preventive war," see Weber, "Power Play: The New 'National Security Strategy.'"

a state's leaders are engaging in a prudential form of moral reflection that requires their actions to be shaped in part by a quest for authorization, in this case, by appeal to the international system (or parts thereof), not by an older, self-authorizing appeal to reason of state. By requiring, at minimum, this form of moral reflection, the international system is expanding the application of the just war criterion of competent authority.

The "Office" of National Power in International Politics

States in the international system have a sense of who they are and what they are to do by reading how they fit into the system and what they are to do about it. In a sense, they play roles. *Role* is a sociological concept that presupposes a set of relationships into which the player fits, and in which it plays a part. Within the international system, however, the role is authored partly by the contours and dynamics of the system and partly by the state itself in the course of pursuing its interests and exercising its power in international politics. In writing about the emergence of India on the world scene, Robert Kagan explores the question of how India begins to perceive its role in the group of great powers and in its neighborhood.[8] What this means is that India is asking not only about its emergent interests seen from within but also about the expectations arising from the international system that shape both its obligations and its possibilities as it occupies its place in the relationships. At the same time it is attempting to discern how it may need to attempt to reshape expectations and power relations in the course of establishing its role.

The metaphor of role is useful, but I prefer to speak of this system-defined and system-enabled set of expectations as the office of national power in international politics. Admittedly, "office" sounds too formal and too fixed, but it also conveys the notions of connected relationships and accountability. Moreover, it reflects the fact that expectations for some states have a high level of visibility and endurance in the workings of the system. There is, of course, nothing precise or neatly structured about this "office." There is no organizational chart, no job description, no mission statement. There is no hiring, no electing, no appointing. What "office" means is that there are ways that a state fits into the international system in terms of its location, history, perceived and actual intentions, and package of capabilities. There are expectations in terms of what other states and members of

8. *The Return of History and the End of Dreams.*

the system anticipate it will do, need for it to do, and hope to prevent it from doing. It refers to behavior that is usual, fairly predictable, desirable, and undesirable. There is nothing about this role or office that implies or requires a neat superseding of national interest by international expectations. The state represents itself, but its ways of pursuing national interests are shaped, redirected and limited by the contours and movements of the international system. The question is, What are we supposed to do, now that we find ourselves in this historic set of relationships, and how do those expectations influence our interests and our behavior? If there is any constancy to the expectations, which usually there is, that constancy of expectations defines the office. It also provides a further application of the criterion of competent authority. The relevant members of the system provided authorization by identifying a need and inviting a prominent state to deal with it.

Tension and Ambiguity

Of course, the constancy of expectations is no guarantee that a dominant state will elect to fulfill them. Precisely because the "office" does not supersede or supplant the fundamental commitment to national interest, the state always will deal with the tensions between system expectations and its own directly definable concerns. In order to take on the responsibility of system-designed office in particular cases, it must become convinced that the more effective operation of the system, enabled in those cases by its interventions, is consistent with and supportive of its own interests. It may opt to decline the invitation, and position itself accordingly.

The further problem is the ambiguity of power translating into leadership. There are two principal conditions for the concept of office in the international system. First, the movements of the system itself design or declare the office, and then point to the appropriate executor. Both the necessity of the office and its authorization arise from systemic events and arrangements, not from policies of particular states. The operative question: What is necessary in this time and situation to make the international system function as an enabling and limiting social mechanism, and which state is best qualified to take the lead? Second, the office is conferred on a particular state because it is the predominant power, and therefore is perceived as the one to deal with the salient issues in the absence of an effective and authoritative international organization. This second condition introduces serious ambiguity into the concept. Once a predominant power has been recognized and acknowledged, it must decide whether to work within the expectations of the system. If it does so, those expectations become limiting concepts. Or it may decide to use its predominant power—specifically its military power—to redesign the system in accord with its own interests and ideology. The reluctant involvement of the U.S. in the Bosnian crisis of the 1990s is an example of the first.[9] The aggressive plan of the Bush administration to restructure the world system for democracy and capitalism, and even to "rid the world of evil," exemplifies the second.[10] The latter was a program for system transformation, not for fulfilling the expectations of an office within the system.

The "Office" of the United States

Often it is said that Britain played, and was expected to play, the role of balancer in the state system of Europe. That role in effect was its "office," so long as the state system worked with a balance of power. Now the United States occupies the preeminent office or offices in international politics. By reason of its status as lone superpower and its placement at the center of the world economy, the U.S. is variously or simultaneously the leader, the policeman, the enforcer, the enabler—or something else defined by interaction between the presence of the United States and the organization or disorganization of the international system. The problem for the United

---

9. The Balkan crisis of the 1990s looked very much like a European problem to be dealt with by Europeans, and therefore not an immediate responsibility of the United States. Some European voices argued to the contrary that the U.S. was the leader of NATO, and in fulfillment of that role should enter the contest to stop the slaughter. Moreover, with its massive and disposable air power it had the material means to control the outcome which other states did not have. Reluctantly, and belatedly, the United States took on the leadership role and brought the conflict to a close, displaying the reality of its unofficial office not only through the efficacy of its military might but also through the work of its special ambassador, Richard Holbrooke, who steered negotiators to a finalizing formula in the Dayton Accords. What the U.S. national interest was in this matter was not immediately clear, unless it was the interest in encouraging the continuing viability of NATO, but there was no doubt that the U.S. was expected to take a leading role (even though the Balkan crisis was, in fact, primarily a European problem).

10. "The National Security Strategy of the United States of America, September 2002." The "rid the world of evil" quote is taken from Bush's remarks in the National Cathedral, Washington, DC, on September 4, 2001. It is cited on p. 5 of the NSS paper. See also "The National Security Strategy of the United States of America, March 2006." My comments on the latter document are Weber, "Exporting Democracy."

States, and indeed for other states, is that this real but unofficial office carries no prescription for decision and action in particular situations. Partly because critical events are multidimensional and dynamic, partly because the office in the system is that of a national state with its own interests, there always is some variable reading of what is to be done, and by whom, and when to do it.

For example, arguments over intervention in the Libyan uprising in March 2011 reflected a conflict between traditional and expanded notions of national interest. According to the traditional concept, the United States should stay out of that conflict, because it has no overriding interest in Libya, its great resources are committed heavily elsewhere, it does not really know who the rebels are, it does not want the complications of military entry into another Muslim state, and it has no clue as to how the intervention might end. The U.S. should simply leave the problem to others and let the struggle in that country work itself out. On the other hand, the U.S. does have an interest because of the involvement of Libya in Mideast, Arab, and Islamic politics, and because of the connection between that web of relationships with the NATO alliance, of which the United States is the leader. This is the expanded concept of national interest, of which I wrote earlier. It illustrates how changes in the international system expand national interests to the point of inviting a concept of office of national power in international politics.

Another argument is that the U.S. occupies a permanent role of leader by reason of its military dominance and economic preeminence. When problems arise in the international system, the U.S. should step in to fix them—without necessarily waiting for support from other countries or authorization from international organizations. In order to be able to do that, and to safeguard its own continuing interests, the U.S. must invest heavily in military preparedness and project power where needed. This view is associated often with "American exceptionalism" and with neoconservative thought. Applied to this particular case, the U.S. should have led and controlled the attack on the Libyan forces from the beginning of the intervention to its successful conclusion, inviting and employing the assistance of others but trusting no one else to take the initiative and sustain it and to do everything right. The U.S. is the permanent leader of the system by reason of its preeminent military and economic power. At this point in history that is what the U.S. is called to do, and it should have done it—by reason of its calling and office. "It is our destiny," as one CNN commentator put it. Senator John McCain, among others, was a strong advocate of this position.

The argument from national interest is set over against this one, but so also is the clear and simple rejection of any office at all in the international system, especially one that would allow and encourage the United States to act expansively and aggressively by reason of its superior power, or to be isolationist—if that is a possibility. The rejection is even more emphatic where the exercise of such a wide-reaching office would involve some uses of military force. Taking on such responsibilities as an enduring feature of national participation in international politics projects national interests into definitions of international interests, burdens national resources to the breaking point, and reflects lack of trust in other peoples to resolve their own problems. It is arrogant, void of serious knowledge of other societies, and often abusive and exploitative. Andrew J. Bacevich's *Washington Rules: America's Path to Permanent War*[11] is a powerful statement of this point of view.

With regard to the Libyan case, Bacevich argued that the history of British and U.S. interventions in the Middle East is one of self-interested actions clothed in moral justifications, and that the interventions have failed. The evidence of events shows that the U.S. should back away from its supposed leadership role, recognize that the Middle Easterners can resolve their own problems, and that history will sort things out.[12] In other words, any "office of national power" is not a systemic obligation of the dominant state but simply a case of ignorant and destructive meddling. Bacevich's objection is a very powerful one, although it does not account for the fact that American power inexorably is caught up in international expectations. The presence and exercise of American power require constructive redefinition and creative guidance, but not a simple denial of their reality and relevance.

There was yet another proposal. It is a significant variation on the *leadership* view of office in the international system. According to this position the United States indeed is the leader and the preeminent power, but it is not the only state or institution with responsibility in the system (or certainly in this area of the world), nor should it be expected always to make the first move and to carry the heaviest load. Leadership in this case consists not only in acting to prevent massive civilian casualties, and to change the balance of forces, but also in encouraging or requiring other

11. Bacevich, *Washington Rules*.
12. Bacevich, "Last Act in the Mideast."

states to define and fulfill their own offices in the international system. Note that this alternative does not imply any rejection of office or leadership, but only a different definition of office and leadership, one consonant both with the resources and other interests of the leader and with the continuing needs of the international system. To put the matter bluntly, the United States would not be under such expectation to assume an office of leadership in such matters if the other NATO members had not cut their military budgets so drastically because of dependence on the United States. The U.S. should lead in such a way as to evoke more shared responsibility and avoid knee-jerk expectations of American initiative. This seems to have been the approach taken by President Barak Obama in executing the U.S. role with regard to Libya.

Criteria of "Office" Responsibility

These examples and their implications suggest some criteria to be taken into account in any theoretical exploration of the nature of such a systemic role and the justification for its operations. 1) The proposed action should be doable and limited. 2) It should be defined within the system itself, not as an alternative to the system. 3) It should receive authorization from other states that recognize the importance of the proposed action and the rightness of the designated leader in undertaking it. 4) Those authorizing or inviting states should provide significant material support for the action, especially in view of their unwillingness to exercise the office themselves. 5) The executor of the office of leadership should be reluctant to undertake the responsibility, unless there is a clear connection to its own national interests defined traditionally. 6) The "reluctant leader" should attempt to work itself out of office, or at least reduce the tendency of other states to call on it for help. It does this by encouraging other member states to accept more responsibility in fulfilling the requirements of the system.

These criteria will help make the concept of office work, if the office is understood by the designated leader to derive in some sense—however rough—from the needs and workings of a developing international system. They will not appeal to a powerful state that wants to redo the system to suit itself. In that case one should ask whether it is not preferable to revert to the exclusive and limiting concept of national interest. Or whether any state, however powerful and highly motivated, really is fit—morally and materially—to attempt to transform the system unilaterally.

Care of the System: From Prudential Wisdom to Stewardship

The expansion and development of the international system result in the growth of organic relationships, tough and thick in some places, fragile and thin in others. The toughness and thickness of the relationships reflect the civilization of power, and therefore the social constraints on resort to war. Where states and societies are integrated more fully into the system, one would expect them to be less inclined to reach for military solutions to their international problems. That is the principal argument for urging and working for the maturation of the system and its greater inclusiveness. It is an argument also for encouraging states to care for the system itself, its stability and problem-solving, and not focus on national interests narrowly defined.

A word of warning: the international system can be nurtured toward greater organic solidarity, but not to the end of a permanent cohesiveness that would guarantee an end to war. Its development is processive, not progressive. There is no automatic upward movement, no prospect of a final state free of conflict by reason of solidifying covenantal relationships. The system remains vulnerable to disruption, and always will so remain. No state or society is defined permanently in its selfhood or ambitions. Large and powerful societies may reach for hegemony and preference, and expect deference and concessions. Emerging and expanding societies will seek to rearrange elements of the system to their own benefit. Rogue states will mount threats, and premodern states will attract Cooper's "defensive imperialism." Some elements, principally terrorists, will seek to destroy or disable what they cannot control. A seemingly mature society may suffer an economic collapse, offering demagogues the opportunity to recover its unity and strength by tyranny at home and aggressive behavior abroad. In short, good things can happen via the systemic civilization of power, but dire risks always will remain. There is no guarantee of progress, no irreversible societal solution, no "end of history."

Both possibilities are predictable when political analysis is supported by an understanding of human nature that underscores its ambiguity. Human beings are capable of fashioning social existence in such a manner as to allow them to live together peaceably, to promulgate laws to regulate their behavior, to create governing institutions to protect them and to enable them to pursue common interests, to assign some degree of predictability to the future that will allow them to establish families and communities and pursue their livelihoods individually or in common. On the other hand, their efforts are never free from the tendencies toward disintegration in human society, driven by latent egoism emerging at times into public and divisive energies.

That is why states that find value in peaceful, cooperative, and relatively predictable relationships must make care of the system a fundamental concern of their foreign policies. Heretofore the basic guide has been national interest. That criterion remains in force, but now it must be read and engineered in the context of the international system or systems of which a state is a member. One implication of the principle of care of the system is the care of bilateral and multilateral relationships, not simply as instruments of the pursuit of national interest, but also by reason of their functional and organic importance for the strengthening of the system itself. Nurturing of these relationships enhances the integrity and supportive, enabling, and limiting capacities of the web of which the states and their connections are members. However, attention to these points does not automatically serve the aim of care of the system. The health and enduring strength of the international system must be a basic concern of policy, along with national interest and the care of relationships.

Another implication is that member states must be aware of, and not only wary of, states that are not members of the system, or not fully committed members. The principle of care of the system begets the further principle of striving to make the system fully inclusive. Thomas Barnett has driven this point home with his distinction between states that are connected to globalization and those that are not. The latter are threats to peace, the former are much less so. Fully inclusive means not only joining up but also coming into fuller possessions of the benefits of an inclusive membership.

Much of what has been said here about care of the system implies prudential motives. That is, states should care for the system and maintain its health and strength because it is in their interest to do so. Of course, that is true. However, what is true also is that as states become integrated into a system, and more and more obligated to care for it, their involvement carries their commitment beyond what is necessary to national interest in a narrow sense, and what the narrow definitions might prefer to allow. At that point membership moves beyond prudence to stewardship. That is, it becomes a matter of trust, of moral responsibility reflecting expectations not reducible to interest alone. When care of the system, and care of relationships, take on this moral quality, the system is beginning to take on the substance of a community.

PART THREE
Peace, Justice, the Church

10

Peace: The Freedom to Be Vulnerable

The end of war is peace; therefore the politics of war moves toward the politics of peace. That should be a cause for rejoicing—and it may be, but not necessarily. Understood empirically and descriptively, any peace that is the outcome of any war is a particular organization of power. It is an arrangement between the erstwhile combatants characterized either by the complete dominance of one over the other, or by relationships of mutuality and reciprocity, or by some combination of the two. Simply as a political concept peace has no inherent normative content. It does not require one to speak of peace with justice, or "development as the new name for peace" (Pope Paul VI), or peace as the benevolent union of hearts and minds, or peace as the harmony of interests, or peace as biblical *shalom*, or peace as the equity of distributive justice. In actually working for and sustaining peace these normative concepts become of great importance, but they do not inhere in the empirical notion itself. When one attempts to bring reconciliation into conversation with war and peace, one must contend with this basic reality.

In this chapter I shall propose a normative understanding of peace, which I see as a possible outcome of the civilization of power, and which represents the ultimate possibility of *pax terrena*. It is peace as the freedom to be vulnerable. To do that I must discuss the concept of peace as an organization of power, relate that concept to peace as the freedom to be vulnerable, and then investigate the prospects for such peace in international politics.

WAR, PEACE, AND RECONCILIATION: PART THREE

Pax Civitas Terrena as a Christian Concern

First, however, I must make clear that in this connection we are talking about that peace which the world gives, not the peace of the city of God. In St. Augustine's Latin terms, it is the peace of the *civitas terrena*, not that of the *civitas dei*. Augustine asserted without reservation that only the latter was true peace. The former was false peace, because it resulted from the love of earthly goods, not from the unlimited, unrelenting willing of the self in love toward God. Nevertheless it is a good that should be sought even by Christians, because it establishes conditions for existence in a fallen and depraved world. Earthly peace is the tranquility of order, not of the order established by God and in relation to God, but of order in a chaotic world that God is not willing to dismiss into nonexistence. Moreover, the peace of the earthly city and the peace of the City of God are not simply set in opposition to each other—they are intermingled in historical existence until the end of time.

Therefore we may proceed with the examination of earthly peace in the context of divine reconciliation, even while recognizing its theological limitations. The concern for and promotion of earthly peace fall under the work of preservation, an essential aspect of the history of God's efforts to renew and redeem the fallen creation. The intermingling of the peace of the two cities is a reminder not only of their differences but also of prevenient grace—of grace intervening in worldly struggles to support and promote healing influences against those that are harmful. As we proceed with this examination of earthly peace we must inquire into the nature of that peace, and ask how best we are to get there—without sacrificing or otherwise offending against the normative directives deriving from God's work of reconciliation in Christ. At the outset, we must examine the reality of peace as an organization of power.

Peace as an Organization of Power

If the concept "peace as an organization of power" seems a bit strained for the usual understanding of peace (if not of power), let us take note of what peace in the larger contexts of conflict actually looks like. We speak historically of *Pax Romana*, *Pax Britannica*, *Pax Sovietica*, *Pax Americana*, and others. Each is a hegemonic regime, deserving the appellation of "peace" not cynically or with approval but by reason of its ordering of conflicting elements over a vast sweep of the earth, combining dominant force with variable—often minimal—degrees of consent. From varying perspectives one can judge them good or bad, or just or unjust, or effective or ineffective, but each properly is called "peace" in an empirical, conceptual sense by reason of being an organization of power effective in its own time and place.

The states of Europe historically have been at war with each other, when not actively then latently by menacing behavior, persistent conflicts of interests, and changes in alliances. At the present time they do not fight, they do not threaten belligerence, they do not engage in arms races with each other. None of them rates as a hegemon, although some are stronger, richer, and more influential than others. They cooperate through the European Union, NATO, and other institutions, combining centralization and decentralization, competing economically and often diplomatically and legally. They eschew the use or threat of military force in their dealings with each other, but retain some military capability for coping with other threats—present or potential. They amass economic power, to the extent possible, but use it to sustain the wider community as well as to support their own interests—not to overpower and defeat their neighbors. Out of a history of war and threats of war they move ahead with a politics of peace. Their peace is different, certainly, from that of the hegemonic and imperial sprawls. It is an organization of power relying mainly on consent and agreement, with a minimal to nonexistent threat of force.[1]

The Meaning of "Freedom to Be Vulnerable"

I have stated that in this chapter I shall propose a normative definition of temporal peace, namely peace as the freedom to be vulnerable. This notion is one possible outcome of the civilizing of power, and as such it fits within the empirical claim that any worldly peace is a particular organization of power. What does "freedom to be vulnerable" mean? It means that

---

1. For a critical reading of Europe's "peacefulness," see Kagan, *Of Paradise and Power*. Of course, my sketch of Europe is woefully incomplete, intended merely to provide an example of peace as an organization of power quite different from that of the dominating heavyweights of history. European consensual power relies at times—openly or implicitly—on the military power of the United States, resenting and criticizing it all the while as the power of an arrogant hegemon. For different reasons it resists the hegemonic pretension of the Russian Federation, which seeks to influence European behavior through control of its supply of natural gas. In neither case, however, is European power, however organized and displayed, an exercise of military power.

one can exist as a human being without material means of defense, and without having to worry about threats to that seemingly defenseless existence. One needs no walls or moats or weapons—especially no weapons. That condition seems a long way from my earlier—nonnormative, descriptive—claim that peace also can be the imposition of order by the strongest party. Unfortunately, that also remains true. However, peace as the freedom to be vulnerable is a temporal possibility, and one to be encouraged and supported by what is learned from the understanding of politics and war in the context of God's work to renew the fallen creation. Such peace is, nevertheless, an organization of power. But its achievement rests on the possibilities of power, and is not simply frustrated by its limitations. Also, it is not dependent on trust in God, even though it becomes a presence in the history of God in relation to the fallen creation.

The leading question is, how can one be free, if one does not have the capacity to threaten or repel? I have specified *material* means of defense, because there are other means of defense that are effective protectors even though they are not weaponized. The most basic is a culture of acceptance that respects individual and communal existence, and provides ways of decision-making supported by the persons for whom and with reference to whom decisions are made. It is a form of social protection that allows the members of the society to go their ways and transact their business because they know that others will neither threaten them nor impede their actions. To put it in familiar terms, it is the social fabric. The model for this is the small town where folks do not lock their doors or post guard dogs. The absence of fear of violation does not rest in the fact that potential evildoers know that the inhabitants are armed, but in the cultural conviction that "here we treat persons and their property with respect and do not take advantage of them." When the social fabric is strong, the members are free to be vulnerable. Their culture and institutions of mutual acceptance and support make it so.

Accompanying this culture of acceptance and supporting it is a moral ethos of trust grounded in the valuing of individual persons, their lives, their property, and their privacy, and in the expectation that such valuing will be reciprocal. We trust one another, we do not harm each other, we support each other. The members are wary of outsiders, because they fear they might not adhere to the same norms, but within the supportive society the members are free to be vulnerable. Obviously, this freedom in a condition of vulnerability is a characteristic of societal existence. It is not something posited of or possible for individuals in a so-called state of nature. It implies membership, social awareness, societal solidarity. Freedom is freedom in association. It is not the liberty of unattached, unrestrained individuals. Nor is it the supposed freedom afforded by arming the members of the society against each other. Proposals to arm the members reflect lack of faith in the social fabric and its supporting moral ethos, and probably also the attempt to replace the freedom to be vulnerable with a social faith of a different kind.

An Organization of Social Power

Let us be clear that this freedom is a form of social power. It is not simple powerlessness, because the social consciousness and social fabric that are of its essence have the power to compel behavior. It is the power of consent, not of force. It is a function of membership. Those who are affiliated members of the group enjoy the protection of its social constraints and expectations. Those who are not members fall under suspicion until they build a track record of acceptance of group norms and practices. The nature of this freedom is freedom in community. It is not unrestrained liberty; it is constrained by group norms, customs, and laws, and by the responsibilities that are reciprocal with the benefits. That is, it is a social experience, not merely a provision for individual activity. One must accept the obligations and restraints of membership in order to enjoy the protected vulnerability that this societal power allows. More forcible forms of power, such as a police force, are not simply absent from this mix, but they are minimal, in uniform, and not visibly central to the community life. The presence and operative influence of this societal matrix is why the freedom to be vulnerable is an organization of power, and why it is authentically peace.

Not Equivalent to Nonviolence

The freedom to be vulnerable is not premised on acceptance of a principled nonviolence. To make nonviolence the commanding principle of action with reference to war or other forms of conflict is to make the peace of Christ the sole relevant form of peace, and to dismiss the role of societal power. The intention, certainly, is to minimize the role of violence in human interaction, and especially in the behavior of states, but that happens in response to the work of God, which requires both preservation and resistance to wicked behavior. The substantive concern is with power, of which violence is a variable element. Nonviolent direct action (which is not the same as principled nonviolence) is a commendable and often preferable form of Christian action, but it is nonetheless an exercise of power, and as such must submit to criteria of justification as does violent power in support of a just cause. The point of achieving the freedom to be vulnerable is to eliminate resort to violence, or at least make it marginal, by virtue of the effectiveness of forms of social power not primarily or directly reliant on violence.

Not Optimism Concerning Human Nature and History

Freedom to be vulnerable also is not to be confused with optimism concerning the inherent goodness of individuals and some supposed basic inclination to be kind and supportive. The social systems and agreements that support such freedom are modes of constraint. They presuppose what theologians call original sin. They are aware of tendencies to unbridled egoism and the maximization of power, and they act both to shame such tendencies and to deflect and suppress their energies. These organic societal agreements manifest the complexity of human nature—the inherent sociality of persons as well as their inclination to pursue their own interests. They allow the pursuit of personal or group concerns while drawing on the needs and possibilities of sociality to guide, enable, and limit the efforts. In other words, they protect the vulnerability that supports and encourages societally supported but restrained freedom. To repeat the point, they require membership. Membership affords security and relative freedom of action to those who accept the rules and other conditions of belonging.

Moreover, there is nothing in the definition of peace as the freedom to be vulnerable that holds any hope of steady progress toward that goal. Peace is a social construction—an incremental product of social willing and achievement, not of any automatic movements in history. What is achieved can be lost. It can be subverted by arrogant expansionism, by economic collapses, by missionary efforts to transform existing relationships to fit an ideal pattern, or by inattention to the necessities of caring for the supportive system. Those who want to move toward a condition of peace as the freedom to be vulnerable must understand the process of movement, must commit to it, and must work to sustain the relational and institutional achievements.

Peace in International Politics

This analytical scheme uses smaller societies as models and illustrations, but it is developed with nation-states and the nation-state system in mind. As we have seen, the state system long has been in transition to a global system, one with different forms and magnitudes of power, more complicated concepts of interest, and problems of global sweep that require interstatal cooperation. For a long time the states themselves have been the basis for thinking about political understanding and also for relationships among the states. Now the international system provides the framework for political analysis, but especially for interactions among the elements of that framework. However, the transition from one system to another is not complete. The state system, with important modifications, remains a principal element of the international system. States still pursue their own interests. They still maintain and nurture their own means of power. On occasion, they still make war, or at least threaten it. But in some ways and in some degrees they must come to terms with the realities of the international system, support its control mechanisms, and even modify their own aspirations. The international system with its existence, promise, and requirements is the context for imagining peace and establishing it.

States wanting to enjoy a degree of vulnerability that allows freedom to focus on internal development—for example, on economic or cultural matters—and not primarily on military security, must become self-conscious members of this international system with its expectations and self-limiting rules. If they decline to do so, they must look to material and related means to defend their vulnerability. They then have freedom only within the allowances of their material power, especially their weapons, which, of course, is their power to limit the freedom of others. Moreover, the states that choose not to enter this self-limiting system rightly are viewed with suspicion by those states that are members. Vis-à-vis these "outsiders" the member states maintain a defensive posture that is at least potential if not actual. This posture testifies to the fact that the members are not free to be vulnerable as long as those outside the system do not join, and in joining accept the terms and constraints. In principle, they are not "at peace."

In addition to this institutional and relational ordering, a second element in the composition of international peace is, as I have indicated, a moral ethos that defines shared values. These values inform and undergird the social fabric that establishes freedom in community. This ethos includes commitment to the community itself and its purposes, and to the importance of having socially defined and established rules governing behavior. It includes also respect for individual members, their property, and their groupings and cultures. Absent this element, the power of cohesion in the society reduces to the values that the rulers and hegemons choose to enforce. Freedom in that case is the freedom to obey or die, but not the freedom to be vulnerable. States and their leaders wanting the freedom to be vulnerable in international politics must commit themselves to these values and to care of the international system, and not only to pursuit of their particular interests.

Historically, the transition from state system to international system has been accompanied by a transition from *reason of state* as the moral determinant of state actions to an ethos of human rights. This ethos embodies both individual rights, leading to democratic authorization and control of power, and group rights, requiring the inclusion in government and the distribution of social goods to groups that heretofore have been excluded, if not oppressed. The presence and influence of this ethos is intended to limit the power of governments internally and their exercise of power beyond their own jurisdictions. Of course, it does not have full and immediate acceptance in every occasion of a government's exercise of power either internally or externally. The authority of this ethos is questioned because of its religious and philosophical origins in Western civilization. It is pushed away by some governments which insist that societies should be left alone to deal with their own problems according to their own internal understandings, norms, and traditions. It comes into conflict with other moral traditions, principally Islam with its insistence on the fundamental authority of *Shari'a* law. Nevertheless, the ethos of human rights makes a fundamental assertion of moral power that governments and other traditions claim to acknowledge even when violating its demands. It is the emergent and active moral ethos of the international system. To honor it, at least in principle, is a condition of membership in the system, and therefore a factor in reaching peace as the freedom to be vulnerable.

Not Equivalent to Disarmament

"Freedom to be vulnerable" is not to be confused with disarmament. It should follow, of course, that members of the community or system find no need of arms to repel threats from each other. But the fundamental condition of freedom is based on the presence of social supports and constraints, not on the absence of weapons. When citizens begin to arm themselves because of a sense of domestic insecurity, it is a sign that the liberating means of social support are losing their efficacy. When some states maintain a significant military establishment despite their friendliness with many other states, that is clear evidence that the international system is not complete and that those who are not members do not experience the comfortable freedom to be vulnerable. If individual states want the freedom to be vulnerable, they must promote the development of social supports and the incorporated ethos, not the spread of weapons.

In international conflict the emergence of weapons competition usually reflects political differences and threats that seem to require military capability for intimidation or protection. That being so, the problem fundamentally is not in the armaments competition but in the political competition. Why do the states want or need an enhanced military presence? The weapons problem will not be solved apart from the resolution of the political problems or other nonmilitary conflicts. To be sure, there are situations in which technological development of weapons systems is so vast and aggressive that technology itself creates new stages of political conflict. That was the case in the burgeoning nuclear stand-off between the United States (with NATO) and the Soviet Union. Even there, however, disarmament was not possible apart from fundamental political changes. The competing states would not agree to disarmed vulnerability so long as they were willing to accept the risks of nuclear war to shield the values or aspirations that their military power was designed to protect. More recent manifestations of developing technological threat and competition are computer hacking assaults on military, industrial, and electrical grids, and the struggle over control of space. The responsive exercises of power may arise from political differences, or at times from economic competition. Freedom to be vulnerable in international politics requires the solution of conflicts as the prerequisite to disarmament, or at least as its companion. Optimally, it requires membership in a community or system that provides societal supports and incentives that reduce dependence on more material forms of coercion or defense. It requires nurturing into existence institutions to house the community, the membership, and the common efforts to draw their efforts toward peace to a solution. That is a work of politics, not of military competition.

WAR, PEACE, AND RECONCILIATION: PART THREE

Peace and International Organization

The international system as a whole is the context for achieving peace defined as the freedom to be vulnerable. The process of forming and solidifying the international system, and therefore of achieving for all peoples the freedom to be vulnerable, is never complete, even when it develops well beyond the presuppositions of the old European state system. Empirically this projection moves in the direction of completion but never reaches it. There is no steady and determined movement from particularity of power concentration to a comprehensive, consenting, authorizing community. A more likely outcome is Robert Cooper's typology of modern, premodern, and postmodern states. Even so, the two persistent realities in international social interaction are integration and disintegration. Nothing in the history of shifts and constellations of power annuls either tendency. In particular, nothing in the way of historical ordering promises to dam up the flows and spurts toward disintegration. The movement toward larger formations based on deepening and widening of consent is a matter of necessity, vision, and will.

The particular inference to be drawn here is that peace thusly defined is not contingent on the maturation, completion, and full authorization of international organization. International organizations are elements in the (much more comprehensive) international system. They are important elements. Many states seek their authorization for their foreign exercises. Some of them, however, will go their own ways without such permissions. Nevertheless, they will be careful to abide by the terms of membership in the international system, unless, of course, they are willing to risk war. The persistent tension between state interest and systemic authorization will continue to test the organic and institutional supports for the freedom to be vulnerable. The prospects for peace are no more promising than the viability of those supports.

Peace/*Pax Terrena* in the History of Divine Reconciliation

The civilization of power leading to the freedom to be vulnerable seems to imply that human history is moving that way and that the continuation of this process leads to permanent peace. Of course, the empirical reality of human history does not support that conclusion. As we have seen, the international system is mixed. The state system remains even while the international system spreads across the world, war seems less profitable to many states, and the benefits and authority of membership continue to grow. This persisting mixture opens important possibilities for world peace, but it also retains the explosive potentialities for disruption of various kinds, especially with the retention of particularity of interest and state control of military power. Also, these development aspects of the international system operate within the persistent tendencies of international society toward a dialectic of integration and disintegration. The contradictions of history can be managed, but never completely eliminated.

None of this is surprising to anyone who reads peace in history as *pax terrena*, that is, as earthly peace allowed by divine grace but without the stability and permanence of the peace of the City of God. Understood thusly, earthly peace of some kind will be possible, but it will be tentative and volatile, always susceptible to collapsing into war. When God is not loved above all things, and all things temporal are not loved in relation to God, the human will is disposed to pursue its particular loves as though they were divine. The idolatrous egoism of national loyalty will claim the religious devotion of its subjects or citizens and will elevate its national goods above the international common good. War always is a risk. When it happens it may be restrained in its ferocity by what Clausewitz termed the "nonconducting medium," but it will not lose the tendency to descend into the logic of absolute war.

The larger theological perspective, of course, is the history of divine grace, moving from the disruption of original creation to the completion of reconciliation in and through Christ. I have contended from the beginning of this work that the history of God in relation to the fallen creation is the context for all human efforts—politics, peace, war. *Pax terrena* is a function of the preserving work of God, and therefore is not self-explanatory. But neither is it static. It is allowed, disrupted, and revised by the dynamic encounter of grace with all human arrangements. Grace moves the formations of earthly peace always toward greater fulfillment of community and rejections of the ways of violence, but always with the understanding that sin remains a potent force for wrecking even the highest and most effective of such achievements. This context is the inclusive framework for Christian thinking about war and peace. Likewise, its call to participate in the divine work is the foundation and substance of the Christian vocation to be a reconciler. Christians must continue to work for peace as the freedom to be vulnerable, and in doing so to promote the civilization of power, but always with these qualifications and reservations.

Thinking About and Acting for Peace

The maximum expectation of peace in earthly terms is the freedom to be vulnerable. It is the highest realization of *pax terrena*. This freedom is a social construction, not a libertarian or individualistic possibility. It is an organization of power, the outcome of the civilization of power. It is an achievement of human beings in temporal fulfillment of the preservative work of God. It anticipates the kingdom of God, but is not itself the kingdom of God. Christians who hope and strive for peace in their world should think in these terms and work to create the social conditions that will enable the freedom to be vulnerable.

11

Justice, Power, and Peace

If peace is described in empirical terms as an organization of power, what can be said of justice? Justice always is included in any normative concept of peace, that is, "no peace without justice." The classical normative combination is *pax, ordo, iustitia*—peace, order, justice. If justice is integral to the normative concept, which includes peace, can it be left out of the empirical description? Does justice correspond in some way to the normative understanding of peace as the freedom to be vulnerable? It does, but that outcome depends—as does peace—on the formation of a social order that brings to expression the original creative elements of divine justice, namely, the identification of human persons as the image of God and the vocation of humankind to care for the creation. To arrive at that conclusion we must give attention to the relationship of reconciliation to the problem of justice in international conflict. But first we must examine the empirical issues of the possibilities for justice to the organization of power.

Justice in the Organization of Power

One may argue in Augustinian terms that there will be at least some minimum of relative justice in even the most unjust order. Without that minimum, the organization of power will dissolve into disorder, that is, into non-being. Or one may argue in terms of practical experience that any organization of power will fail over time if there is not at least some degree of consent, and that consent will not be given without minimal satisfaction of justice to those consenting—beyond, that is, consenting simply because they want to exist and not be destroyed. Practically speaking, some element of justice, however small, cannot be left out of the organization of power, and therefore out of the composition of peace.

The fundamental question, however, is not whether there is some minimum of justice in the organization of power, but whether the element of justice present in the organization of power is significantly determinative of the empirical reality of peace. What is the substance of that element of justice, and who defines it? Can one locate a scrap of justice in the rule of Joseph Stalin over the Soviet Union and its satellites, or of Saddam Hussein over Iraq? Possibly—to satisfy a theoretical point, or even to complete a political analysis. But whatever looked like justice in either case was there not because it was just but because the rulers made some useful concessions to buttress their uses of force to suppress the population. Whenever Stalin suspected any person or group of persons of pressing for treatment different from what he defined as justice, he would respond by exterminating them. Saddam Hussein did likewise, imitating Stalin. The subordinated people got the point. What determined the organization of power in those cases was not the will to embody justice in the society but the will to rule by force.

Clearly that is not the same as saying that justice is an organization of power. Justice is present in different ways depending on how societal power is organized. When society is organized into the peace of superior force, the dominating ones determine the meaning of justice and how it is to be allotted. When society is organized to allow and encourage widespread participation, justice emerges as a social product of consent and competition. That mode of organization allows also for the formation of a societal consciousness that shapes common ideas of what justice means, and establishes the moral basis for competition and for the revision of accumulations of power and privilege. Justice is a variable component of the organization of power, but not inherently definitive of it. It is not a name one puts on the organization but a reflection of the changeable arrangements of force and consent.

The problem of defining justice, and of the role of justice in peace as the organization of power, becomes visible in a different way where warring parties battle over competing concepts of justice. Looking from the outside, one may contend that justice should be the constitutive element in peace between Israelis and Palestinians, between Catholics and Protestants in Northern Ireland, between India and Pakistan in Kashmir, between Sunni and Shi'a in Iraq. However, on examination one sees that the opposing sides have different and usually contradictory ideas of what justice entails, and how it should define a political or military settlement. Justice is not an ideal that hovers above the struggle, coercing or nudging combatants toward a "just" solution; it is what the struggle is about.

If the force of one side prevails overwhelmingly, that side will decide what justice means in the resulting relationships. The losers will not accept the prevailing interpretation of justice, but they will be forced to accept the results of the contest of arms. In the meantime, they will nourish their own convictions and plan ahead—possibly pressing for minimal and incremental gains, possibly girding themselves for a messianic turning of the tables. If on the other hand neither side has the power to prevail, and the outcome is more or less a standoff, the resulting peace will be a deal in which both sides agree to a practical definition of justice that conforms to the limits of their power. The deal is the mutual expression of consent in the face of exertions of power that cannot win unilaterally. It is what justice means in the context of the new organization of power. It is a point of arrival in the movement from war to politics.

This deal may not be permanent, because it is what the contestants have to settle for—not what they really want. It is what they have to live with, at least for a while. Moreover, the deal has built-in instability. It is pressed constantly by expectations and claims put on hold for a time but never surrendered completely. And it will continue to be challenged by transcendent renderings of justice—human rights, natural law, prophetic biblical notions, historic memories of other occasions and other times, international legal covenants—that are factors either of emerging international customary and legal standards or of movements toward expectations of justice in the common consciousness of what vaguely is termed "world opinion." Therefore it may not last, and it will be subject to revision either by shifts in power relations or by changes in common consciousness of antagonists who have reached a stalemate and established a *modus vivendi*. But for the moment it is the reality of justice in the organization of power. In Reinhold Niebuhr's terms, it is rough, partial, tentative, compounded with injustice. In Augustine's terms, it is the relative justice of the earthly city, always something less and other than the justice of the City of God.

Does History Move toward Ideal Resolution?

Having described peace empirically as an organization of power, and justice as a particular but unstable resolution of the power struggle, the question arises whether there are any elements of dynamism in the mix that drive both peace and justice toward more ideal resolutions. Is the power that organizes peace increasingly acceptable and authoritative by reason of increasing consent, and does it bring a beneficent and representative ideal of justice with it, or does justice continue to be an ethic imposed by force? Does the "deal" that embodies the empirical definition of justice remain what the prevailing power allows, and the limits of what the subordinated peoples can achieve, or is there some inherent thrust toward a configuration of justice more reflective of the consent of those who cannot enforce their own demands and expectations? Is there dynamism inherent in history that moves recalcitrant parties toward some ideal fulfillment despite their willing to the contrary?

One possible answer simply in descriptive terms is that historically changes in the arrangements of both peace and justice largely are what considerations of prudence allow in the administration of power. The leaders of the Roman Empire, for example, were conscious of the prudential value of justice and were intentional in incorporating it into their exercise of power over non-Roman peoples. They wisely allowed some authority of local law and custom under the overall sovereignty of Roman law, as well as appeals to Stoic political ethics and the rights of Roman citizens, thereby disarming to a useful extent the resistance to Roman military rule. However, the Roman legions were the ultimate guarantors of the order that defined peace as well as of the positive order of justice. Without getting into the debate over the causes of the fall of Rome, one can argue confidently that they had more to do with material factors from within and without than with any supposed inner dynamism toward liberty and justice. In international conflict, the desire for security and for attending to other matters may prompt contending parties to arrange peace and adopt practical standards of justice that require the curtailment of their ambitions. In either case, the motivation is practical wisdom, not commitment to ideals of justice. Given different counsels of prudence, other conditions may result.

But is there something in the restlessness of the human spirit that presses and aspires toward a tranquility of order more reflective of the desires of subordinate peoples than legions and military forces prefer to allow? Does it find expression in the civilization of power, in the transition from force to consent as the principle of organization of power? On the surface the "Arab Spring" looked like the dynamism of the human spirit, finally claiming its moment and autonomy and moving forcefully—even if nonviolently—to break the shackles of tyrannical power. However, the political process of consent allowed the Muslim Brotherhood to claim electoral victory and impose a repressive religious ideology, thereby negating the liberating values of the uprising. That in turn was succeeded by a return to military rule. It is possible that the drama has not played itself out. We know that liberating ideas, once released into the stream of public awareness, tend to have a power of their own to command attention and often to present a rasping mandate for implementation. Critiques of racial oppression, the subordination of women, and the maldistribution of wealth in a society, to cite some examples, all created an agenda for pressure on the prevailing organization of power and a demand for implementation. But for the present, neither the movement toward consent to power nor the force of liberating ideas has produced the result desired by the rebels for liberty. The liberating ideas themselves must become the substance of the ethos undergirding the organization of power. Only then will they rate as the public standard of justice.

And of course there are other factors. Peoples under the press of military control often prefer the known realities and costs of that rule to the uncertainties of chaos. The wandering children of the Hebrews protested to Moses that they would prefer to return to the material security of the fleshpots (cooking-pots, with meat in them) of Egypt under Pharaoh's repressive rule than continue on their increasingly difficult trek to freedom under the rule and guidance of Yahweh. Ideational factors ultimately may triumph, but if they do so it will be through their command of a new organization of power, and not merely because they represent a thrust of the human spirit whose time has come.

Limits to a Consensual Organization of Justice

The conclusion is twofold. First, the civilization of power, known also as the politicization of conflict, can in fact produce a societal condition that for the society is the meaning of justice. This condition is embedded and expressed in the ethos that supports the authoritative order of society. Within this order, supported by this agreement as to the meaning of justice, the members are at peace because they are relatively free to be vulnerable. In this sense, justice is the organization of power and the definer of peace. Second, the stronger the commitment to the ethos the more the members of society are convinced that this portrayal of justice represents more than merely the predominance of power through consent. Where this happens the meanings of justice come to have an authority of their own—one not reducible to prudential calculations. These results may be real and they may be highly beneficial, but they do not escape the sociological reality that the ethos of justice depends fundamentally on the character of the organization of power.

Such apparently progressive results may be possible for smaller, more compact societies, but they do not reflect the status of an ethos of justice in international society, and will not for the foreseeable future. As we have seen, the movement toward an international system of rules and memberships is overlaid on a system of states of various size, power, and interest. These states and state factors exist in persistent tension with any emergent and ambitious international ethos. Added to the mix of political tensions are the divergent understandings of justice resident in the various religious cultures on the world scene. The result is that there is no ethos of justice to control the organization of power and establish confidently the freedom to be vulnerable. Certainly there is none with a definite authority of its own, one not reducible to prudential calculations. An ethos of human rights has become highly influential, but it is very far from being the sole, authoritative, and compelling order of justice.

Theological Contributions

If we submit this problem to theological probing, we may be resigned to accept nothing more promising than Augustine's justice of the earthly city—a residue of order arising from the misdirected loves of material goods in a world that has departed from the authenticating love of God. As we have observed, however, even that result is not worthless. It is a provision of divine grace for a world that otherwise would destroy itself. Christians, Augustine asserts, should pursue that good for the earthly city, although it is not and never will become the full justice of the City of God. Yet even that acknowledgment is valuable, for two reasons. One is that it reminds us that no earthly political scheme—and especially no warring efforts—can produce the perfect justice with which to organize societal power. History can and may see improvements, but it will be brought to an end only by divine intervention, not by human political or military means. No "final solutions," messianic programs, historical dialectics, religious conquests, or other sweeping measures can bring to fulfillment a redemptive ending or new creation. These possibilities belong entirely to divine providence. Another is that it testifies that the grace of God continues to press against all temporal achievements of justice, especially the false and oppressive ones, and to submit all human efforts to the discipline of the reconciling work of God. Every achievement of justice in the earthly city stands under the judgment of God, with the hope for gracious renewal.

But are there more substantive possibilities for defining justice? There are, and they are drawn from the righteousness of God manifest in the original plan of creation. First, humankind, male and female, is the image of God. This humanity of individual persons must be elevated above historical identities—national, racial, cultural, class, religious, gender, political. Christian witness always must protest against the dehumanization of the different and the hostile. Second, all peoples are called to tend the garden, that is, to care for the creation God has given to all of us. Many states are coming to realize that all of us have a common human habitat, that global climate change, the purity of the air we breathe and the water we drink, the prudent use of resources, the linkage of deforestation with global human welfare, and other similar or related issues are both national and common human interests. That awareness has a prudential, not a theological basis, but it corresponds to and is reinforced by the biblical understanding of stewardship of creation.

Beyond theses contributions is the ultimate provision from the justice of God: the repudiation of god-making, or the divinization of groups—national or otherwise—competing against each other in martial conflict. God alone is God. States require a kind of loyalty for their struggles, but what is rendered to Caesar cannot be what is rendered to God. Political devotion always is limited by divine sovereignty. Unlimited political loyalty is unjust, by definition.

It is not the place of Christians to ask whether the biblical definitions of justice are acceptable in the conflicts of the international system. It is their place to witness to the divine order of justice, known to them by grace through faith. Their critiques of god-making tendencies, their affirmation of human identity as image of God and of the common stewardship of creation, may make common cause with more secular and prudential considerations, and in doing so may have a profound influence on any emergent ethos of justice. But the primary test of their efforts is not in possible beneficial results but in their faithfulness to divine justice in the history of reconciling grace.

12

Rethinking the "Just War Ethic"

The just war ethic—or *justified war* ethic—is a moral instrument for assessing the rightness of resort to armed force for the resolution of conflicts, and also of the moral limits of the means used in resorts to martial force. It carries with it a reminder of the residual persistence of justice in the fallen condition of humankind. Some elements of the ethic are pre-Christian in their appearance in the history of moral thought about war, but the development and maturation of the ethic to its present forms reflect its passage through the wandering and conflictive course of Christian political thought. Through that process it has become the principal non-pacifist means used by Christians to investigate moral responsibility for resort to war and to set moral limits to the conduct of war. Through that process also it has acquired some theological substance that shapes the meanings and ends of its components.

In the introductory chapter to this book I stated that I was not writing another treatise on the just war ethic. My concern, rather, was to ask how Christians should think about the problem of war. That commitment remains true, even and especially in this chapter on implications of my approach for just war thinking. The concern in this case is to ask whether and how one should think differently about the just war ethic, once one has established the contextual frames of reference I have presented. If one engages war critically and systematically in the context of the divine history of creational redemption, does such contextualization affect the concept and application of this mode of moral thinking? I am convinced that it does, and I intend to show how that is the case.

A *Political* Ethic

First, the approach developed here requires that the just war ethic be understood and applied in the context of politics. It is, fundamentally, a *political* ethic—an inherent element in the moral administration of power. It is not a device imported into the political process to set things straight, morally speaking, only at times when it becomes needful and relevant. The ethic is a constant element in thinking about the responsibilities of power, about whether power serves justice, peace, the right distribution of resources, the care of creation—or some other set of goods. The alternatives to its political presence are, first, the dismissal of any moral responsibility for the exercise of power, and second, some definition of goals and criteria drawn exclusively from that exercise itself. The first alternative is a withdrawal to what some would call political irrelevance. The second allows the main monitor of applied force to be the concept of reason of state—all exercises of power are justified or rejected depending on whether they serve state interests. The inclusion of the just war ethic in moral reflection on war denies both alternatives. It insists on responsibility for all uses of power, especially power as violent force. It implies an appeal to goals and limits not reducible to interest and superior might. As an inherently politic ethic, it is embedded in all phases of the processive pattern: politics to war, politics in war, from war to politics.

In the first phase of this pattern—politics to war—it is manifest as moral reflection on proposals to change (or maintain) existing inter-statal arrangements. What is there about the existing organization—or disorganization—of power that makes it objectionable and requires that it be changed? What cause justifies the movement from politics to war, that is, to the use of such extreme means—those that signal an end to diplomatic negotiations? What is the intent of those who commit the state to war? By whose authority is this transition undertaken? Is there reasonable hope of success? Will the probable benefits outweigh the costs—almost certain to be heavy, and to all participants? Have all other means of resolution been exhausted? These questions express the familiar just war criterion of *ius ad bellum*, or justification for resort to war. The "resort" criterion is applied primarily in this phase of the sequence, although it has implications also for the entire process.

The second phase of the process—politics in war, or the politics of war—is the time of actual conflict. It is the principal locus of the criterion of *ius in bello*, or what morally may be done in the exercise of armed and destructive force. The governing principles for this criterion are proportion and discrimination. The former allows doing only what is necessary to achieve military objectives, and nothing more—and, of course, it counts the costs. The latter designates what morally never may be done, regardless of whatever advantages may accrue to the attacking force. The most common and prominent specification of this limit is that noncombatants never may be directly and intentionally attacked, for the purpose, that is, of furthering the cause of war or speeding up its termination by killing the civilian population. Including this criterion implies that if there is no moral guidance of this sort, that is, no moral limitations, then the logic of war rules. Anything may be done that serves the purpose of achieving victory and winning the war.

The limiting criterion of proportionate damage applies also to one's own resources, and not only to limiting so-called collateral damage to noncombatant populations. One recalls in this regard the contempt Stalin is said to have felt for Eisenhower in World War II, because Eisenhower was committed to limiting the damage that might be done to his own forces, also, and not simply to accepting massive casualties if they were necessary to destroy the enemy. In Stalin's view, soldiers as instruments of war were as dispensable as intervening civilian populations as the cost of victory. Eisenhower was intent on winning, but also on cutting the losses among his own soldiers. The *ius in bello* criterion requires the curtailing of all unnecessary losses, and not only the exclusion of noncombatant populations from direct and intentional attack.

To place the criterion of *ius in bello* in this phase of the process means only to indicate its primary locus of application. It is active also in the phase of "from politics to war," and not only in the conduct of war. Anticipations of limits to weapons and tactics are elements in the considerations of resort to war, as was evident in the debate over the role of nuclear weapons in the prospects of war between the United States and the Soviet Union. The same is true in moving from "war in politics" to "from war to politics." How the weapons and tactics are used may influence greatly the nature and quality of the peace that should follow. That is to say, the conduct of war involves the prospects for peace, which often are influenced greatly by the manner in which a war is fought. It has been said (by Woodrow Wilson, among others) that the making of war should be disciplined by the intention to promote peace. A defeated enemy may be far less manageable if it has suffered devastating and humiliating consequences on the way to the end of conflict.

The point of these comments is to illustrate the nature of the just war ethic as a *political* ethic. The criterion of *ius in bello*, like the ethic as a whole, is a limiting and constructive element of power. It is not an alien set of norms imported from some idealistic realm to confuse the martial pursuit of interest. However, it requires a substantive reconceptualization of the political context itself, in that it manifests a moral—and even a religious—commitment not native to the so-called "logic of war" and the unrestricted use of power in pursuit of interest.

In further consideration of the move "from war to politics," the change in this case is to a new organization of power. Here one expects some degree of dominance of the victor over the vanquished. However, the victorious power should guide the peace settlement in such a way as to evoke the creation of a new order of relationships—one in which the vanquished will have the status of a participatory even if somewhat subordinate actor, not that of a population permanently under the harsh control of a new overlord. I have called this process the civilization of power—a movement from disconnected force to institutionalized means of decision and consent.

The just war criterion of just intention works in this political context to encourage an organization of power that is organic, institutionalized, and participatory. It is concerned especially to avoid the kind of conduct of war, and imposition of peace settlement, that will create resentments and irredentas[1]—incentives for subsequent war-making. *Just intention*, which intends peace of a justifiable sort, must guide the transition from war to politics. These conclusions further establish the nature of the just war ethic as a political ethic.

The Full Context of History

Second, the contextualization method of this approach places the just war ethic in the full setting of the history of hostilities. Just as this ethic is by nature a political ethic, so also it is a factor in a particular political history. Moral reflection in every stage of a conflict, but especially in "from politics to war," requires thorough attention to what Alan Geyer has called

---

1. Irredentas—literally "unredeemed"—are territories appropriated by the victors that the vanquished believe are rightly and historically theirs, and for the recovery of which they may be motivated to fight later on.

the "burdens of history."[2] That is, it calls for honest attention to the long-term development of the conflict, and especially to any responsibility the "wronged" state may bear in creating the problem at issue. "Just war" reflection should not begin only at the point where one side believes it has been given "just cause" to initiate hostilities but should take into account the long-term reciprocity in the relationships of the combatants.

According to John Howard Yoder, a "punctiliar" view of the moral process too often is characteristic of just war reasoning. It focuses on the particular moment of judgment, not on the previous history leading to the conflict, and sees only one side in the wrong.[3] These complaints about the ethic are justifiable, but only when it is not employed as a *political* ethic. If it is regarded and used thusly, its application works in the movement from politics to war, and therefore is attentive to the full prehistory of the conflict. In that case, the side claiming justification has at best only a qualified claim, assuming that its own interests and actions made some contribution to the conditions of conflict. Its justifiable appeal may be to nothing more than a compromise, and not to a justifying victory. Also, its claim to justifiability may be fraudulent—a judgment revealed in the history of the conflict. The uncovering of why things actually happened the way they did may require repentance and self-correction, and not justify resort to war.

Relocating the Criterion of "Just Intention"

Third, another consequence of this approach is the relocation of the criterion of just intention to the position of primacy in the just war ethic, supplanting the criterion of just cause. The main reason for this change is that just intention is the criterion connected most directly and integrally to the full process of political experience, and therefore is the one that makes just war reasoning a type of political ethic. Just cause as the starting point for moral analysis is vulnerable to the charge of John Howard Yoder, noted above, that the "just war paradigm" is "punctual" in its construction, in that it works from a particular point in history, not with the longer and wider history itself. Of course there must be a justifiable cause, but identification of causes arises out of the constitutive political history. To take the *cause* issue as the beginning of moral reflection is to ignore the breadth and depth of congruent factors creating the occasion for conflict. The criterion of just

2. Geyer, "Just War and the Burdens of History," 135.
3. Yoder, "Just War Tradition," 295.

intention, as I shall show, makes that historical connection. Moreover, the criterion of just intention excludes some kinds of causes before the current issues of conflict even arise. It rules out such possible causes as territorial aggrandizement, military glory, and vengeance.[4] In that respect, at the outset, it is preliminary to just cause.

How does the criterion of just intention make this historical connection, and how therefore does it identify just war moral inquiry as a political ethic? What is truly dominant in the notion of a just intention is the intent to produce peace, and thereby to transcend the rule of military means. Peace, as I have insisted, is a particular organization of power. War is the transition from one organization of power to another. The transition involves reliance on military means, but the new organization suppresses such means. This process is the one identified earlier: politics to war, politics in war, from war to politics. The role of intention is present in every stage of the process, and especially in the design and promotion of a new organization of power—that is, of a new arrangement of peace. In this role it quite obviously is a *political* ethic.

In the execution of this work of moral reflection just intention requires the employment of all the other criteria—cause, authority, cost/benefit, reasonable hope of success, and those asserting moral governance of the conduct of war. It is therefore the organizing criterion for the use of all the other criteria in moral reflection on the interrelated issues of war and peace. In this regard as in others it displaces just cause from primacy. The implication is clear: to consider the justice of resort to war and the conduct of war, place this consideration in the context of peace, that is, in thinking about a just reorganization of power.

The Just War Ethic in Theological Context

For the most part, this reconsideration of the just war ethic has drawn on implications of placement in its political context, identifying it specifically as a political ethic. In what way or ways is the theological context consequential in this reconsideration? First and most obviously, theological insight influences the definition of peace. As I have argued, peace as a reorganization of power relations emerging from war can be either a peace imposed on the vanquished by the victor, with no concern for rights, freedom, or welfare, or a peace defined as a cooperative result with consent

---

4. On the exclusion of vengeance, see my "Vengeance Denied, Politics Affirmed."

subordinating the rule of force. Any notion of peace shaped by reference to the divine work of reconciling the fallen creation will move relations toward the latter type. It will encourage and assist the formation of institutions and ethos that establish a new international order with ambitions to allow the freedom to be vulnerable.

Moreover, it will embody the fundamental elements of original creation that must come to expression the more the divine order is reflected through the civilization of power. One of these is the recognition of human beings as image of God, as human persons whose imaging nature always should be a check on arbitrary power, who rightfully claim to share in the consensual creation of the social milieu they will inhabit, and whose being and rights will be protected therein. Another is the enactment into policy of the task given to these image-creatures, namely, to be stewards in common of the habitat with which God has entrusted them. The reorganization of power that defines peace after war must acknowledge this common responsibility and not limit itself to consideration of interests, boundaries, and reparations.

And of course, any theological influence will remind all participants that any new arrangements will be formations of *pax terrena*, not the peace of the City of God. Military force, however clearly justified, does no more than produce a new organization of power. It does not bring in the kingdom of God.

This reconsideration of the justified war ethic is both an effect and a requirement of Christian thought about war in the context of the divine history of renewing and reconciling the fallen creation. It demonstrates the integral, not the accidental, character of this means of moral reflection on the uses of power. It shows that this moral reflection involves a political ethic but is not therefore a purely secular ethic. The theological claims drive it to seek justice above the logic of pure war, to define peace in ways that serve reciprocity and the subordination of violent means, to value the lives of all persons related to the conflict in any way, and to enjoin all parties to engage the divinely given vocation to care for the earth. This not a checklist of criteria to be acknowledged when considering war. It is a profoundly serious exercise of moral-political responsibility. And because of its historical grounding, it may require repentance, forgiveness, and transformation of perceptions and policies.

13

Reconciliation, War, and the Church

The goal of Christian thinking about international conflict is to see an end of war as an instrument of policy, and of violence as an instrument of international engagement. The end of war, of course, is peace. As we have seen, however, peace is a particular organization of power. The concept of peace to which we have come in this inquiry is that of peace as the freedom to be vulnerable. It is an organization of power in the sense that the strength of community in its organic relationships of law, institution, and ethos supports the common life and subdues the egoistic tendencies toward aggressive self-seeking and the imposition of will. Under these conditions, the members of the society are free to be vulnerable in that they rely on the protections of societal power and not on their own forcible means of protection. When these conditions prevail in international society, there will be no inclination to resort to war and consequently no resort to instruments of violence. The task of Christian thinking about war and peace therefore is to define and contribute to the creation of these societal conditions. It is not simply to renounce war and violence.

Of course, these conditions do not prevail in international society as a whole. What we find instead is a mixture, as Robert Cooper describes it, of premodern, modern, and postmodern states. International society is in transition from a Europe-centered system to a global combination of interconnecting institutions and expectations with states that range from very weak to super-strong. There are systemic links that states affirm and benefit from most but not all of the time, and self-conscious and self-defined political centers that ignore or manipulate the system when it suits their perception of their own interests. Such peace as is generated by this mixture is an organized/unorganized system of power. In some ways and in some circumstances states feel free to be vulnerable, but always with a degree of reservation to act unilaterally to defend or pursue their own interests. There is cooperation on common tasks, but with implicit privilege to go their own way if they feel compelled to do so. For many relationships the means of violence are "off the table," but they remain nonetheless as a residual arsenal for intimidation or action.

The further element of reality in this picture is that it is not going on to completion. The international system never will be such a confident organization of consensual power as to allow its members to pursue their various interests—common or particular—without some option of military backup. An international police force may serve some useful common purposes, but it never will replace the inclination of at least some of the states to act militarily at their own discretion. The theological explanation for this lack of desired completion is that the kingdom of God in its fullness will not come in human history, and clearly not by political and military means. Only the grace of God can overcome the disruption of creation in which humankind fashions finite gods to provide the security and meaning it has lost. This theological insight is confirmed by empirical evidence from the reading of political history that reveals the ongoing dialectic of societal integration and disintegration. There is nothing in political experience to suggest that this dialectic will come to an end, whatever the patterns of positive change may be.

As I have argued previously, however, this ultimate pessimism should not undercut proximate efforts for peace. Theologically, the *pax terrena* is the arena of God's work of preservation. To work for even marginal improvements is to enter into and cooperate with the divine work. Politically, the prospects for peace and therefore the reduction of impulses toward war are implied in the growth and maturation of an international system that states want to join and nurture because they see membership to be in their interests. To join the system and to nurture it implies the acceptance of its rules of behavior, and therefore the setting aside of military action as an attractive means of settling international disputes.

Where to Start?

The important point, however, is not to declare and advertise the ends sought, or even to validate the efforts for peace, but to discern the reality of the present, and in doing so to discover the processes and steps for moving ahead. That takes us to the question of the starting point of faith-filled inquiry. At first glance, the starting point would seem to be war itself. The immediacy of conflict, or its near prospect, is what seizes attention and provokes thought and action. As we have seen, however, no war is an event of its own creation, production, and self-interpretation. War is a function of politics, of the movement from politics to war, to war against but within politics, and again to politics described empirically as the shaping of peace. It takes place within and is an expression of the international system with its historic changes. Therefore the starting point for thinking about war is not the conflict itself but the governing and explanatory political context.

However, the political context may be the starting point for non-theological political and moral reflection, but not for Christian inquiry. Christian thinking about anything, and therefore about war, must begin with a defined theological position, with a faith perspective grounded in awareness of the presence and promise of God, and especially with the work of God in Jesus Christ. From that point one can begin to inquire into the nature and the challenges of war in its historical expression as a political phenomenon. This perspective will describe to us the human condition in the history of the divine-human relationship. It will explain why war is a god-making activity, why it absolutizes causes and tribal memberships, why it transforms and dehumanizes human identities, why it reduces and refocuses the common and corporate calling to care for the earth. It will warn us of tendencies to promote political programs in general and wars in particular as desirable and final solutions to humankind's problems. In the course of this critical function it will disclose the positive norms and values of human being. It will reveal God and not particular states to be the ultimate judge of all being and doing. It will validate group existence projects where they are justifiable, but expose them as proximate and not ultimate values. It will discern the image of God in every culturally formed personal identity, and remind competing groups of their common membership in the family of God and their common responsibility for the stewardship of creation. It will declare the vision of God and the peace of God to be the end and aim of human history, and in doing so will demythologize and dismiss the messianic fantasies that often are the motors of militaristic policies.

The further significance of the theological starting point of reflection on war is in the claim that war and its political context exist fundamentally in the theological context. The one is within the other; they do not exist side by side. This comprehensive reality of the context-within-the-context is the reason why political investigations of the sources and nature of war are necessary to the theological enterprise. Among other considerations, it allows the resolution of the contradictory logics of war and reconciliation. It shows how the processes of both contexts move toward the creation of community with its implication of the subordination of violence to more organic and institutional means of conflict resolution. It directs the redefinition of peace from the imposition of superior force to the societal achievement of the freedom to be vulnerable, and it underscores the central reality of preservation in the execution of the divine work of peacemaking.

Moreover, the theological starting point is the source and substance of the call to Christian life as servants of God. It is the place to encounter war as a problem of Christian faith, and to do so necessarily, inasmuch as war is the most dramatic and destructive evidence of human disruption of God's creation. It should be clear then that for faith-inspired inquiry into war the starting point is Christian belief and the commitment in faith. The argument set forth in this book is that this perspective, this interpretive guide, this definer of Christian vocation is the history of God's work in renewing the fallen creation. Even more explicitly and substantively, it is the divine work of reconciliation—above all its culmination and full expression in God's presence and action in Jesus the Christ.

In Review: How to Think

To review: the central question of this book is, how should Christians think about the problems of war and peace? The proposal is that they must use two contexts of analysis, one theological, the other political. The former is fundamental, because it defines the self-understanding and work of the church, and therefore the life and mission of Christians. Moreover, once the theological context is established, the political context—including war and peace—is understood to fall within it. This theological context is the history of God's relation to the creation, from the uncorrupted design of original creation through its fall into rebellion and disruption to its redemption in the life, death, and resurrection of Jesus Christ. Following the Pauline text in 2 Cor 5, we refer to this history comprehensively and inclusively as the divine work of reconciliation. The necessary inference is that Christians must do their thinking about international conflict under the rubric of reconciliation and war.

However, to assert the priority and necessity of the theological context is not to say that the political context is of minor importance. It is after all the setting within which war appears, and its configurations and demands give war its character and rationale. In its function in human society, not only through its expression in war, it provides abundant evidence of the disruption of original creation. Moreover, the political context of war generates questions about human experience that theological inquiry is forced to face, not in order to demonstrate its relevance but to pursue its vocation under God. For these reasons, at the least, investigation of this apparently secular context is essential to theological thinking about war.

Churches and Their Appropriation of This Approach

At this point, let us pause to insist that there is no exclusive linkage between reconciliation and war, in the sense that the mission of reconciliation is called to mind only when the threat or reality of war requires it. The reconciling ministry is what God has called us to be and to do. The Pauline assignment is clear: God has given us the *diakonia* of reconciliation. Whatever the church does—in worship, preaching, prayer, music, evangelism, pastoral care, service to others, personal and social ethics, education, leadership, stewardship, environmental concern, sacrifice, inclusiveness— is an exercise in the ministry of reconciliation and must be understood and interpreted in that framework. In this respect every congregation is a "reconciling congregation," because the wholeness of its ministry, not some special cause, defines and justifies its existence. Engaging the problems of war and peace is but another aspect of that ministry. Because war and politics fall within the history of God's gracious work, attention to war and peace is both necessary and proper. There is nothing about it that is esoteric to Christian practice. Christians are called to be reconcilers in all aspects of life. War and peace are among the unavoidable aspects.

Having made that point, let us address some of the particular ways in which churches should absorb and exercise this method of engaging conflict.

Peace and Security

What do churches have to offer to their surrounding and inclusive society, based on their self-understanding as ministries of divine reconciliation?

The most important thing they have to offer is the witness to peace as the freedom to be vulnerable—an understanding of peace that derives from their commitment to share in the work of healing in all fractured relationships, from personal to international. This witness compounds the safety of supporting institutions and the reinforcing moral expectations of a common ethos, even though it rests ultimately on the peace of God. This is not a vision of peace projected from ideals unrelated to actual experience, nor is it an "alternative community" (a notion that implies sectarian distinctiveness), nor is it a kind of security achieved by having a weaponized congregation.[1] It is a social ordering achieved in real time and space by folks who do not need protection from each other because they are freed from concerns for personal safety by common beliefs and by institutions that embody those beliefs. It is both an example of what is possible for human beings living together and a proposal for social transformation. In principle it is applicable to international relations as well as to the renewal of neighborhoods and cities.

To be sure, it has a theological foundation for its particular organization of freedom, but its exemplary value does not depend solely on its common faith. The desire for the freedom to be vulnerable can rest simply on prudential reasons for desiring it. States do not have to convert to a common religious belief to want peace defined in these terms. They may build institutions of mutuality and accept legal and moral limits on their behavior and aspirations because they want to pursue interests other than conquest or because they no longer can afford high expenses for military security. The initial contribution of the faith-based example is to show what peace as an organization of power can mean and that it can be achieved. For the churches, it is what we must be and do.

Preaching the Reconciling Word

When President George W. Bush began the invasion of Iraq in 2003, a pastor announced from his pulpit that several ministerial colleagues had phoned to ask what he was going to say about the war. His reply: "Nothing!

---

1. Churches that invite their members to bring guns with them to congregational gatherings are sending a different message. The Christian message is not adherence to nonviolence, but whether the churches want to project a concept of peace based on armed defense, or one based on the solidarity of the community as members meeting together in the presence of God.

Members of the congregation are divided on the issue, and most of them know more about it than I do. I shall say nothing!" His assumption, I supposed, was that if the preacher were to "say something" about a major public event, it would take the form of a political statement—a commentary, and either a validation of the action or a prophetic denunciation. I thought rather that it should be a theological statement—not in the form of searching the Bible for relevant texts, but as an inquiry into the meanings and implications of this development in the light of the biblical message. After all, he was preaching to a worshipping congregation, who expected to hear a message of Christian illumination. He was not called to offer political analysis or advice. How does this event, which seems to open a chasm before us, speak to our faith and demand a response?

As I have argued, the comprehensive message of the Bible is the reconciling word—the history of grace pursuing the recovery of the fallen creation. In the case of entry into war, as in all other cases, one should preach this reconciling word. Preaching that word in its biblical fullness means that God is in the conflict—present and active, not absent or external. God's reconciliation creates a theological framework in which to think about what has happened and is going to happen. In this framework one can raise the issue of the direction of gracious intervention: God intends the healing of the nations, not the victory or defeat of any of the participants. God presses toward the recovery of community, beginning with small connections and developing them to create the possibilities of peace—first as restraint, then as cooperation. One also can detect in grace the direction to move in conflictual relations from reliance on violent means to exploring the possibilities and limitations of diplomacy, and with that illumination to press the possibilities. Also, in this framework one can discern human identity as image of God latent in the historic identities of the opponents, but active as possibilities for transformation.

This framework in essence is the history of God in relation to the fallen creation, and especially the redemptive and renewing character of that history in Jesus Christ. The listening congregation should be invited to see in the developments some things that are not made evident in the evening news, in statements by political and military leaders, or even in the spreading industry of books sure to follow the action. They should be prompted to remember that the intention of God is the healing of the human community, not the victory of one side over the other. They should recognize in their faithful memories the true humanity of all participants as image of God, and not value the lives of "our people" more highly than those of the enemy of the moment. They should acknowledge, as did Abraham Lincoln, that all parties to the conflict are "under God"—and to be under God means in the first instance to be under divine judgment, not to be established on high with divine approval—and that this location under God is a call to confession. They should disabuse themselves of any notion that it is possible to "rid the word of evil" by any political or military means. If all nations and states are under the judgment of God there is none that bears no guilt, and none that is free of participation in the injustices of the world. They should know that no military action of one side or the other will establish the kingdom of God, that "settlements" favoring one side or the other are transitory and come immediately under critique for the elements of injustice and coercion they embody.

One can redesign the elements of the framework. However, the point is that preaching in response to cataclysmic situations that shake and distort all temporal certainties should employ such a means for interpreting these threatening and demanding realities, and the framework always should be directed by the full message of the Scripture. Lacking such a Christian means of interpretation, members of the congregation may be inclined to fall in line with nationalistic fervor, or to accept the guidance of media commentators of one ideological bent or another, or simply to flail around in uncertainty. Preachers without such means may pass by on the other side, with nothing to say and no spiritual guidance to offer. It is essential, in such challenging circumstances, to explore through preaching the meaning of the reconciling word.

Let us be clear, however, that the reconciling word is not an occasional message brought up by war or any other event that seems to shake our certainties. It is the constant theme of all preaching, the context and content of every sermon. This is not to say that every sermon should be on the same topic with the same predictable outline. It is to say that the essential message should come forth in every exposition of every text, in every public proclamation of the Word of God. After all, the good news is that the deliverance manifest in Christ is the outworking of the history of God in relation to the fallen creation. The congregation should know this gracious context of proclamation and hear it as the interpretive principle in every instance of preaching. When the preacher confronts the problem of war, the members of the congregation then should be able to recognize how they are to understand and deal with the problem in faith. The particular issue may be new and provocative, but the message of divine activity and divine grace is the same.

War and the Holy Communion

Often it is said that Word and Sacrament are an essential combination in Christian worship. The practice is more characteristic of some Christian denominations than of others, although all of them should take the proposal seriously. However, the question usually is directed to liturgical practice, and not to broader issues of the problems of human history. What follows from our inquiry thus far, and especially from questions of the self-understanding of Christian experience in history, is that even the Holy Communion is pertinent to thinking about war. In this regard, Word and Sacrament are together in drawing their meaning and power from their roles in explaining and dramatizing the work of God in renewing the fallen creation, in which war is a painfully present element.

The tendency in the experience of the Holy Meal often is to individualize its summons and benefits. As a pastor who many times has officiated in this service, I know full well that both officiant and communicant encourage this tendency. And they should. Receiving the elements is for the forgiveness of sins, the renewal of life, the transformation of the sinner through the body and blood of Christ. It is for me, and for my sins, and for my future life in Christ. That certainly is true, but it is not all that is true. There are social dimensions to the experience. For one thing, the act takes place in the community of believers. Christ is present "where two or three are gathered together." For another, the gifts and the sacrifice are "for the sins of the whole world." We are not allowed to forget that the work of God in Christ is for the redemption of the entire creation. The bread that is broken and offered is indeed the body of Christ, and the blood that is shed is his blood—given for us. But the breaking and the bleeding are the presence of Christ in the whole creation. They call for the renewal of the sinner, but also for the reconciliation of all that God has created and that has been disrupted by sin.

It follows, therefore, that war and all its accompaniments are present in the offering of this sacrament. War occurs in human history, and therefore in the history of God with humankind. It offers visible and terrible evidence that the body is broken, the blood is shed. The sacrament offers forgiveness for the sins of war, as for all sins, through the grace and mercy of God. Its invitation is to the individual believer to draw near with faith and receive the peace of God, but also for the whole world to seek the peace in which all will be free to be vulnerable. Sacrament and Word together attest to this divine reality, and together bring it dramatically and powerfully before the community of faith. When we offer or receive the elements for the renewal of our souls, and pray for reconciliation with our neighbors, we must pray also for the peace of the world.

Church-Political Action through Statements on War and Peace

My original impulse for setting forth on this inquiry into Christian thinking about war was prompted by my reading of church-sponsored statements on war and peace, most of which responded to particular, highly threatening developments in world politics. All of them were abundant in their concern for peace, the renunciation of violent means, and the healing of the nations. Some of them were admirable representations of their theological and ecclesial traditions, and highly knowledgeable in their understanding of the political conflicts they addressed. Others, however, were deficient in their theological groundings and in their perceptions of the realities of political conflict. Those of the latter type were less likely to be taken seriously by the political actors addressed, and not apt to nurture the faith and encourage the action of their own congregations. Therefore I pressed myself to explore the fundamentals of Christian thinking about war, which then might inform the public political speech of responsive churches.

Based on that inquiry, the first recommendation I offer to those composing war-peace statements on behalf of Christian communions is that they declare the theological basis for what they are proposing, and that they expound the basis from a considered understanding of biblical faith. After all, they are speaking on behalf of the church, not simply as interested members or officials who happen to feel strongly about what is occurring in the world of nations. Moreover, they should ground their theological perspective in the work of God on behalf of the fallen world, not in optimistic and progressive views of human nature and history, and clearly not in defensive or—even worse—messianic commitments to the "exceptional" role of their own country. They should hold fast to proclamation of the reconciling work of God in Christ, and therefore to the church's own vocation to join and expend itself in that reconciling work. They should call the church and the world to recognize the image of God in every human creature, and reaffirm the common and universal stewardship of all that God has created. In all of this they should recognize that their proposals are for a world not fully reconciled, with its fragility and disruptive tendencies, and not for a world to be fully reconciled by the adopting of correct policies and procedures—that is, by anything less than the full effectuation of the grace of God.

And of course, there is the political context. Church statements need not have the authority of political experts, but they should be sufficiently aware of what is going on to speak theologically and ethically to the issues, and not offer critiques and proposals that can be dismissed easily as unrealistic and irrelevant. To begin with, they must recognize that prospects for armed threats or conflict reflect political differences. These differences are what must be addressed primarily, not the prospective or actual resort to armed conflict. During the times of grotesque, reciprocal nuclear threats, I heard learned lectures on the counter-position of weapons systems and the grim scenarios of nuclear destruction, but seldom did these lectures work analytically on the reasons for the nuclear architecture, and the ways in which the underlying conflicts might be worked out. Why not? Possibly because it is easier to expose the dangers of the weapons systems than to addressed profoundly complicated issues of political opposition and anger—and their resolution. Or maybe for some other reason. In any event, future attempts at such statements must concern themselves with the realities of political conflict, not with alarmist representations or ideal solutions.

One of the realities is, as I have insisted, that peace is a particular organization of power. What has the organization been in the recent past, why has disorganization set in, and what are the prospects for a new pattern of organization, that is, for a new historic reality of peace? Does any proposed statement suggest possibilities for reorganization, and specifically, any that show real prospects for historical achievement? In this regard, one must note that changes in the organization of power often are the reflex of changes in the international system. I have discussed changes from a Europe-based state system to one that is global and based on different systemic elements. Are the preparers of the statements fully aware of these changes and their implications?

These are issues of political context to be acknowledged and confronted as churches and their authorized spokespersons prepare statements encouraging peace among the nations. Nevertheless, theological self-understanding is primary. It requires the political context to understand fully the empirical aspects of human activity under reference, but the theological witness must maintain its primacy as it works through political meanings and alternatives in discharging its vocation for peace.

Concluding Reflections

The basic task of this book has been to ask how one should think about war as an inquiry of Christian faith. I have answered by arguing that Christians must think about war in the context of reconciliation. The basic reason for this claim is that all Christian thought and action must start from a revealed understanding of the work of God, which in biblical disclosure is the gracious divine activity of renewing, healing, and developing the disrupted creation. The full and final understanding of this work is given with the presence of God in Christ—the reconciliation of the *kosmos* alienated from the source of its being, but restored to right relationship with God in a process of reconciliation yet to be completed. This process is the venue of Christian vocation. It provides the framework for the church's message to the world, for proclamation of the divine Word, for interpreting and activating the power of the Holy Meal, and for informing the public political speech of the churches. It is the context for understanding and responding to war.

I have argued further that in thinking about war the fundamental theological context must engage the political context of war. Christian thinking must understand the dynamics of conflict and learn to recognize both the continuing disruptive tendencies and the institutional and moral elements of community building. By doing so, it discloses the historical and human character of all violent disputes and neutralizes the argument that the logics of war and of reconciliation are in fundamental opposition. It also answers the charge that reconciliation is an end-time dream with no relevance for the present, and that it has no concrete understanding of what war really is about. It opens the possibilities for peace in the divine provision for *pax terrena*, for the real—and not inflated—possibilities for *pacem in terris*.

The reality of war is that it is an engagement on the plane of human history that must be analyzed with political and historical methods, but is never known fully and rightly until it is interpreted in the light of divine disclosure. The dual contexts, with the priority of the theological, constitute the method for Christian thinking about war. It is essential, of course, to put forth Christianity's commitments to peace and love in the course of this inquiry, but it is not sufficient. Peace, as we have seen, is a particular organization of power. The nature of that organization is a theological challenge. Love is defined by the nature and action of God. War is a problem of God before it is a problem of love, and it is a problem of love because it is a problem of God. One should think about God in order to think—in faith—about war. That is both necessary and possible, because war in essence is a theological problem. It is a god-making enterprise in its empirical expressions, and it is disruptive of the plan of God for the whole of creation and especially for humankind. Moreover, the kind and course of divine action decide the general questions of Christian belief and vocation, and in consequence the ways in which Christians understand and approach the problems and challenges of war.

In advancing this method I have not dismissed other approaches, such as the Christian ethic of justified war, the rejection of violence, the following of the way of Jesus, or the problem of sin leading to the role of the state authorized to use force. Each plays an essential role both in assessing the problem of war and in defining Christian response. If I differ with some of the more pacifistic options, it is in defending the role of preservation in the historical work of peacemaking and reconciliation. My central claim is that Christian thinking about war, as about anything else, must begin with God, with the activity of God to redeem the fallen creation, and therefore with God's work of reconciliation in human history and in Jesus Christ.

Bibliography

Aldrich, Virgil C., and H. Richard Niebuhr. "Is God in the War?" *The Christian Century*, August 5, 1942, 953–55. Reprinted with permission in *War in the Twentieth Century: Sources in Theological Ethics*, edited by Richard B. Miller, 56–62. Louisvile: Westminster John Knox, 1992.
Atack, Iain. *The Ethics of Peace and War: From State Security to World Community*. New York: Palgrave Macmillan, 2005.
Bacevich, Andrew J. "Last Act in the Mideast." *Newsweek*, April 3, 2011, 48–49.
———. "The Tyranny of Defense Inc." *The Atlantic*, January/February 2011, 74–79.
———. *Washington Rules: America's Path to Permanent War*. New York: Metropolitan, 2010.
Bainton, Roland H. *Christian Attitudes toward War and Peace: A Historical Survey and Critical Re-evaluation*. Nashville: Abingdon, 1960.
Barnett, Thomas P. M. *The Pentagon's New Map: War and Peace in the Twenty-First Century*. New York: Putnam's, 2004.
Bell, Daniel W., Jr. *Just War as Christian Discipleship: Recentering the Tradition in the Church rather than the State*. Grand Rapids: Brazos, 2009.
Brzezinski, Zbigniew. *Power and Principle: Memoirs of the National Security Advisor, 1977–1981*. New York: Farrar, Straus and Giroux, 1983.
Bultmann, Rudolph. *Theology of the New Testament*. Vol. 1. New York: Scribner's, 1951.
Clausewitz, Carl von. *War, Politics, and Power*. Translated and edited by Edward M. Collins. Chicago: Henry Regnery, 1962.
Cooper, Robert. *The Breaking of Nations: Order and Chaos in the Twenty-First Century*. New York: Atlantic Monthly Press, 2003.
Dudziak, Mary L. *War Time: An Idea, Its History, Its Consequences*. Oxford: Oxford University Press, 2012.
Elshtain, Jean Bethke. *Sovereignty: God, State, and Self*. New York: Basic Books, 2008.
Falconer, Alan, ed. *Reconciling Memories*. Dublin: Columba, 1988.
Fukuyama, Francis. *The End of History and the Last Man*. New York: HarperCollins, 1992.
———. *State-Building: Governance and World Order in the Twenty-First Century*. Ithaca: Cornell University Press, 2004.
Geyer, Alan. "Just War and the Burdens of History." *The Christian Century*, February 6, 1991, 135.
Hauerwas, Stanley. *Against the Nations: War and Survival in a Liberal Society*. Minneapolis: Winston, 1985.
———. "Pacifism: Some Phlilosophical Considerations." *Faith and* Philosophy 2 (1985) 99–104.

BIBLIOGRAPHY

Howard, Michael. *The First World War.* New York: Oxford University Press, 2002.
Huntington, Samuel P. *The Clash of Civilizations and the Remaking of World Order.* New York: Simon & Schuster, 1996.
Kagan, Robert. *Of Paradise and Power: America and Europe in the New World Order.* New York: Knopf, 2003.
———. *The Return of History and the End of Dreams.* New York: Knopf, 2008.
Kissinger, Henry. *Does America Need a Foreign Policy? Toward a Diplomacy for the Twenty-First Century.* New York: Simon & Schuster, 2001.
———. *World Order.* New York: Penguin, 2014.
Long, William J., and Peter Brecke. *War and Reconciliation: Reason and Emotion in Conflict Resolution.* Cambridge: MIT Press, 2003.
Mead, Walter Russell. *Power, Terror, Peace, and War: America's Grand Strategy in a World at Risk.* New York: Knopf, 2004.
Miller, Allen O. *Reconciliation in Today's World.* Grand Rapids: Eerdmans, 1969.
Miller, Richard B. *War in the Twentieth Century: Sources in Theological Ethics.* Louisville: Westminster John Knox, 1992.
Morgenthau, Hans. *Politics Among Nations: The Struggle for Power and Peace.* New York: Knopf, 1948.
"The National Security Strategy of the United States of America, September 2002." http://nssarchive.us/national-security-strategy-2002/.
"The National Security Strategy of the United States of America, March 2006." http://nssarchive.us/NSSR/2006.pdf.
Niebuhr, H. Richard. "War as Crucifixion." *The Christian Century*, April 28, 1943, 513–15.
———. "War as the Judgment of God." *The Christian Century*, May 3, 1942, 630–33.
Niebuhr, Reinhold. *Moral Man and Immoral Society.* New York: Scribner's, 1947.
Nye, Joseph S., Jr. *The Paradox of American Power: Why the World's Only Superpower Can't Go It Alone.* New York: Oxford University Press, 2002.
O'Donovan, Oliver. *The Just War Revisited.* Cambridge: Cambridge Universtiy Press, 2003.
The Project for a New American Century. "Rebuilding America's Defenses: Strategy, Forces and Resources for a New Century; A Report of the Project for the New American Century, September 2000." http://www.informationclearinghouse.info/pdf/RebuildingAmericasDefenses.pdf.
The Proposed Book of Confessions of the United Presbyterian Church in the United States of America. Philadelphia: Office of the General Assembly, The United Presbyterian Church in the U.S.A., 1966.
Ramsey, Paul. *The Just War: Force and Political Responsibility.* New York: Scribner's, 1968.
———. *Speak Up for Just War or Pacifism: A Critique of the United Methodist Bishops' Pastoral Letter "In Defense of Creation".* University Park: Pennsylvania State University Press, 1988.
———. *War and the Christian Conscience: How Shall Modern War Be Conducted Justly?* Durham: Duke University Press, 1961.
Ross, Dennis. *Statecraft—and How to Restore America's Standing in the World.* New York: Farrar, Straus and Giroux, 2007.
Runyon, Theodore, ed. *Theology, Politics, and Peace.* Maryknoll, NY: Orbis, 1989.
Stassen, Glenn H., ed. *Just Peacemaking: Ten Practices for Abolishing War.* Cleveland: Pilgrim, 1998.

BIBLIOGRAPHY

———. *Just Peacemaking: Transforming Initiatives for Justice and Peace*. Louisville: Westminster John Knox, 1992.
Sturzo, Luigi. *Inner Laws of Society: A New Sociology*. New York: P. J. Kenedy, 1944.
Sun Tzu. *The Art of War*. Translated by Thomas F. Cleary. Boston: Shambhala, 1988.
Thielicke, Helmut. *Theological Ethics*. Edited by William H. Lazareth. 2 vols. Philadelphia: Fortress, 1969.
Thompson, Kenneth W., ed. *Moral Dimensions of American Foreign Policy*. New Brunswick, NJ: Transaction, 1984.
Toynbee, Arnold J. *War and Civilization*. New York: Oxford University Press, 1950.
United Methodist Council of Bishops. *In Defense of Creation: The Nuclear Crisis and a Just Peace*. Nashville: Graded Press, 1986.
United States Conference of Catholic Bishops. "The Challenge of Peace: God's Promise and Our Response." A pastoral letter on war and peace by the National Conference of Catholic Bishops, May 3, 1983. http://www.usccb.org/upload/challenge-peace-gods-promise-our-response-1983.pdf.
Vatican Council II. *Gaudium et Spes (Pastoral Constitution on the Church in the Modern World)*. In *Proclaiming Justice and Peace*, edited by Michael Walsh and Brian Davies. Mystic, CT: Twenty-third Publications, 1991.
Voegelin, Eric. *The New Science of Politics*. Chicago: University of Chicago Press, 1952.
von Rad, Gerhard. *Holy War in Ancient Israel*. Translated and edited by Marva J. Dawn and John H. Yoder. Grand Rapids: Eerdmans, 1991.
Waltz, Kenneth Neal. *Man, the State, and War: A Theoretical Analysis*. New York: Columbia University Press, 1954, 1959.
Weber, Theodore R. "Christian Realism, Power, and Peace." In *Theology, Politics, and Peace*, edited by Theodore H. Runyon, 55–76. Maryknoll, NY: Orbis, 1989.
———. "Exporting Democracy." *The Christian Century*, July 11, 2006, 10–11.
———. *Foreign Policy Is Your Business*. Richmond: John Knox, 1972.
———. "Guilt: Yours, Ours, and Theirs." *Worldview* 18 (1975) 15–22.
———. "Law, Change, and Reconciliation." *Religion in Life* 47 (1978) 46–61.
———. *Modern War and the Pursuit of Peace*. New York: Council on Religion and International Affairs, 1968.
———. "Patriotic Legislating in the Context of Grace?" In *God and Country? Diverse Perspectives on Christianity and Patriotism*, edited by Michael G. Long and Tracy Wenger Sadd, 225–40. New York: Palgrave Macmillan, 2007.
———. "Power Play: The New 'National Security Strategy.'" *The Christian Century*, March 8, 2003, 26–29.
———. "Reconciliation as a Foreign Policy Method." *Religion in Life* 38 (1969) 40–54.
———. "Security, International Responsibility, and Reconciliation." *Quarterly Review* 6 (1986) 12–29.
———. "Theological Symbols of International Order." *Journal of Church and State* 29 (1987) 79–99.
———. "Thinking Theologically about International Development." In *The Making of an Economic Vision*, edited by Oliver F. Williams and John W. Houck, 189–216. Lanham, MD: University Press of America, 1991.
———. "Truth and Political Leadership." The Presidential Address to the Society of Christian Ethics in the United States and Canada. *Annual of the Society of Christian Ethics*, 1989, 3–19.

BIBLIOGRAPHY

———. "Vengeance Denied, Politics Affirmed: Applying the Criterion of 'Just Intention.'" *Societas Ethica Jahresbericht/Annual*, 2000, 170–76.

Wesley, John. "Justification by Faith" (Sermon 5). In *The Works of John Wesley*, edited by Albert C. Outler, 1:181–99. Nashville: Abingdon, 1984.

———. "National Sins and Miseries" (Sermon 111). In *The Works of John Wesley*, edited by Albert C. Outler, 3:566–76. Nashville: Abingdon, 1986.

Wolfers, Arnold J. *Discord and Collaboration: Essays on International Politics*. Baltimore: Johns Hopkins University Press, 1962.

Woodward, Bob. *Shadow: Five Presidents and the Legacy of Watergate*. New York: Simon & Schuster, 1999.

Yoder, John Howard. *Christian Attitudes to War, Peace, and Revolution*. Edited by Theodore J. Koontz and Andy Alexis-Baker. Grand Rapids: Brazos, 2009.

———. "Just War Tradition: Is It Credible?" *The Christian Century*, March 13, 1991, 295–98.

———. *The Politics of Jesus*. Grand Rapids: Eerdmans, 1972.

Index

acceptance, culture of. *See* culture of acceptance
Afghanistan, war in, 74
Africa, 102
Alexander the Great, 90
alliance politics, and war, 72
Al-Qaeda, 106
ambiguity of power, 111–12, 116–17
"American exceptionalism," 113–14
amity and enmity, 64*n*10, 71
anthropology, Augustinian, 38–40
"Arab Spring," 136–37
Aristotle, 58
"asymmetrical warfare," 83
Atack, Iain, 10*n*11
Atatürk, Kemal, 76
Atlantic Community, 95
Augustine, 38, 122, 135, 138
authority, 107–10
avoidance of particular wars, 62

Bacevich, Andrew J., 79*n*11, 84*n*4, 114
Bainton, Roland H., 10*n*8
balance of power, 82, 95
    "for freedom," 98–99
Balkans, crisis in, 112
Barnett, Thomas P. M., 17, 78, 92–94, 101, 104, 117
bases, military, 79
Bell, Daniel W., Jr., 10*n*10
"bent to sinning," 63
Bosnia, crisis in, 112
Brecke, Peter, 12, 14*n*16
Britain, 112, 114

Brzezinski, Zbigniew, 36*n*6
Bultmann, Rudolf, 31
Bush, George W., 72, 108–9, 112, 152

Caesar, rendering to, 56–57, 139
capitalism, 62, 99, 112
care
    of creation, 40, 139
    of the international system, 116–18
Carter, Jimmy, 2, 78*n*10
cause, just. *See* just cause
Cheney, Richard, 98*n*8
children of God, 35–36
China, 15, 77, 86–87, 96, 102
Christ
    in God's work, 149–50
    peace of, 125–26
    and preservation, 53, 55
    and reconciliation, 29–32
    and suffering, 49–51
    and war, 155–56
church and reconciliation, 151–58
City of God, 122, 131, 135, 138
civilians, casualties of, 47, 142
civilization of power, 64, 89–100, 116
    and justice, 137
    and *pax terrena*, 132
civitas, 89–91
civitas dei, 122
civitas terrena, 122
Clausewitz, Carl von, 16–20, 69–72, 73*n*7, 80, 131
"coalition of the willing," 98–99, 108–9

165

INDEX

coercion, 7, 81. *See also* force
Colombia, 15
combatants and noncombatants, 47, 142
commander in chief, 75–76
Communion, and war, 155–56
community, 4, 152
   international, 91–93, 117–18
consent
   vs. force, 21, 58–60, 82, 91–94
   in the international system, 109
   and justice, 137–38
consequences of war, 42–44
Constitution, U.S., 75–76
contexts
   of war, 16–23
   of "everything else," 78–79, 92–93, 101
   theological vs. political, 148–51, 152
conversation between war and reconciliation, 21–22
Cooper, Robert, 71*n*4, 94–100, 102*n*2, 107, 116, 130, 147
cooperation, and grace, 59–60
creation
   care for, 40, 139
   fallen vs. new, 35
   and God, 28–30, 32
criteria for the leadership office, 115
crucifixion and suffering, 49–51
crusades, 56, 65
culture of acceptance, 124

damage, proportionate, 142
deal, justice as, 135–36
deal-making, vs. reconciliation, 33–34
defense, means of, 124
dehumanization of war, 43
democracy, 99
"democratization of power," 91–92
derangement, of powers, 76–78
destruction, vs. preservation, 60
deterrence, 84–87
diakonia of reconciliation, 151–58

diplomacy and politics, 71
disarmament, 85–87
   vs. vulnerability, 128–29
discernment, 45, 51
   contextual, 4–5
disintegration and integration, 36, 63, 130
dislocation. *See* disruption
disruption
   the fall as, 40
   of the international system, 116
   of society, 48–49
   war as, 42–46, 61
divisions, and war, 44
domestic politics, and war, 71–72
dominion. *See* care, of creation; image of God
duality, of the fundamental vs. existential, 41–42

economy and the military, 79
Ecuador, 15
Egypt, 87, 137
Eisenhower, Dwight D., 79, 142
elements of national power, 82–83
Elshtain, Jean Bethke, 18*n*4, 70*n*2
enmity, and amity, 64*n*10, 71
ethos
   of human rights, 128
   of justice, 137–39
   of trust, 124–25
Europe, 14, 147, 157
   peace in, 15, 33*n*5, 95–99, 123
   state system of, 3, 80, 102, 112, 130
European Union, 123
"everything else," context of, 92–93, 101
"exceptionalism, American." *See* "American exceptionalism"
experience
   vs. fundamental reality, 41–42
   vs. possibility, 61–66

fall, the, and redemption, 28–29

INDEX

flood, the, and God's preservation, 52–55
"following Jesus," 5–8
force, 7
   vs. consent, 21, 58–60, 82, 91–94
   and justice, 134–35, 142, 146
Ford, Gerald, 78n10
forgiveness, and reconciliation, 31–34
freedom
   human, and the flood, 52–53
   to be vulnerable, 121–32
Fukuyama, Francis, 62n9, 104
future, the, visions of, 65

Geyer, Alan, 143–44
Ghadafi, Muammar, 106
globalization, 17, 103, 127
   and the civilization of power, 92–94
God
   and pacifism, 7–8
   as redeeming war, 9–10
   suffering of, 51
   work of, 3–4, 20, 29–32, 149–50
Gospel, and preservation, 54–55
government, power of, 56–59
grace
   and judgment, 51
   prevenient, 30–32
   as reconciliation's context, 5, 19–21
   See also history of grace
groupings, social, 44
guilt, collective, 47–48

Hauerwas, Stanley, 7
Hebrews, 137
history
   and an ideal resolution, 135–37
   and just war ethic, 143–45
   vs. logic, 21–22
   and peace, 126, 131
   possibilities of, 61–66
   as war's context, 18
history of grace, 10–11, 19–23, 27–37
   consummation of, 61–62
   and historical salvation, 65–66
   and justice, 139
   and *pax terrena*, 131–32
   in preaching, 153–55
   and preservation, 53–60
Holbrooke, Richard, 112n9
human identity, 41–43
human rights, 128
humans
   identity of, 41–43
   idolatry of, 38–40
   nature, 63, 126
   role of, 3–5
Huntington, Samuel P., 14n17
Hussein, Saddam, 4, 134

identity, human. *See* human identity
idolatry, 57, 131, 139
   war as, 38–40, 42–43
illumination, and public events, 153
image of God, 3, 5
   and justice, 139
   and just war ethic, 146
   in preaching, 153–54
   recovery of, 30, 32, 35
   in the theological context, 149
   and war, 40–44
imperialism, 90, 122–23
   "defensive," 96–97, 107, 116
inclusiveness, in the international system, 105, 107–8, 117–18
India, 15, 87, 96, 102, 110, 134
innocent, the, suffering of, 48–50
institutions, international, 102–3
insurgents, 83
integration, 36, 91–94, 117
   vs. disintegration, 63, 130
intention, divine
   in creation, 40–42
   just (*see* just intention)
   preservation as, 60–61
intention, just, 11, 143–45
interest, national. *See* national interest
International Atomic Energy Agency, 87
internationalism, Western liberal, 94

INDEX

international system, 14–15, 72–73, 80, 101–18
  and nuclear weapons, 86–88
  and peace, 127–30
Iran, 15, 78n10, 83, 86–87
Iraq, 87, 134
  war in, 4, 72–74, 108–9, 152
Islam, 62, 76, 90, 94, 99, 113, 128, 134
isolationism, 114
Israel, 15, 87, 134
ius ad bellum, 10, 84, 141
ius in bello, 10, 47, 84, 141–43
iustitia, 133

Japan, 33n5, 87, 102
John Paul II, 85n5
Jones, Major, 34–35
judgment, and war, 45–51
just cause, just intention, 143–45
justice, 133–39
  divine, vs. divine mercy, 55–56
justification, and reconciliation, 31–32
"just peacemaking," 64–65
just war ethic, 10–11, 64, 80, 84, 107–10, 140–46

Kagan, Robert, 15, 103, 104n4, 110, 123n1
Kashmir, 15, 134
Khan, A. Q., 87
King, Martin Luther, Jr., 4
kingdom of God, 6–7, 56
Kipling, Rudyard, 90
Kissinger, Henry, 102n1
Knox, John, 33n5
Korean War, 77
kosmos, 30–31, 37, 53, 159
Kuwait, 4

leadership, of the United States, 112–15
LeMay, Curtis, 84n4
Libya, 106, 113–15
Lincoln, Abraham, 76

logic
  of reconciliation, 16–23
  of violence/war, 16–23, 69–70, 79–80, 143
Long, William J., 12, 14n16
love, and pacifism, 7–8
Lutheranism, and the order of preservation, 8–10, 54

MacArthur, Douglas, 74, 77
Manichaeanism, 50–51, 56, 65
McCain, John, 75n8, 114
Mead, Walter Russell, 83
mercy, divine, vs. divine justice, 55–56
method
  analyzing contexts as, 22
  vs. contextual discernment, 4–5
  theological vs. political, 11–12
Middle East, 87, 102, 106, 113–14
Míguez Bonino, José, 1
"military-industrial complex," 79
modern state, 95–99
modus vivendi, 135
Moltmann, Jürgen, 1–2
moral reflection, and just war ethic, 141, 145–46
moral responsibility
  and just war ethic, 140–41
  and nuclear weapons, 84–85
Morgenthau, Hans, 82–83
Moses, 137
Musharraf, Pervez, 77
Muslim Brotherhood, 137

"National Security Strategy," 97–100
nations, and power, 82–83
national interest, 105–17
NATO, 72, 106, 112n9, 113–15, 123, 129
Niebuhr, H. Richard, 49–51
Niebuhr, Reinhold, 2–3, 57, 135
Noah, and God's preservation, 52–55
"nonconducting medium," 18–19
nonviolence, vs. vulnerability, 125–26
Northern Ireland, 134

INDEX

North Korea, 15, 83, 86–87
nuclear weapons, 14–15, 95, 104, 129, 134, 142, 157
    as relational power, 84–86
Nye, Joseph, 82–83, 104

Obama, Barack, 2, 75n8, 115
obedience, and pacifism, 8
O'Donovan, Oliver, 10n9
office, in the international system, 110–15
"office" of national power, 112–15
officers, civilian vs. military, 75–76
optimism, vs. vulnerability, 126
order, societal, and war, 39n1
order of preservation, 8–10, 54
order of redemption, 54
ordo, 133
organization, international, 130
organization of power, 133–39, 143–46, 157–58

pacifism, 7–8, 64
    vs. reconciliation, 20–21
Pakistan, 15, 77, 87, 134
Paul, on reconciliation, 29–32
Paul VI, 121
pax, 133
Pax Americana, 122
pax civitas terrena, 121–22
Pax Romana, 122
pax terrena, 130–32
peace
    as the freedom to be vulnerable, 121–32
    and grace, 59
    and justice, 133–39
    and just war ethic, 145–46
    as organization of power, 82, 87–90, 98–100, 121–32, 157–58
    political requirements of, 74
    promotion of, 61–66
    vs. reconciliation, 16
    and security, 151–52
    as war's goal, 73
Peace of Westphalia, 82

people, will of the, 108
persons-in-community, 91
Pharaoh, 137
police, role of, 92
policy, and theology, 11–12
polis, 89
politics
    international, 127–28
    and just war ethic, 141–44
    and reconciliation, 20–21
    vs. theology, 22–23
    as war's context, 19, 69–80, 149
Politik, and war, 69–70, 75
postmodern state, 96–100
"Powell Doctrine," 71–72
power
    ambiguity of, 111–12
    civilization of, 63–64, 89–100, 116
    of God, 34
    governmental, 56–59
    meanings and problems of, 81–88
    organization of, 65, 121–39, 143–46, 157–58
    relational, 83–86, 99
    social, 125
    "soft," 82–83, 104
    substantial, 83–85, 99
    and war, vs. reconciliation, 16
power, military
    authority for, 107–10
    vs. civilian, 76–78, 92
    and the state system, 104
"power politics," 82
preaching, the reconciling word, 152–57
preemptive war, 109
premodern state, 96, 107
preservation, 81
    as God's work, 52–61
    order of, 8–10
    and *pax terrena*, 131–32
preventive war, 109
psychology, Augustinian, 38–40
"punctiliar" view, 144

INDEX

race, reconciliation of, 34–35
Ramsey, Paul, 2n3, 10n9, 85n5
realist political theory, 1–2, 95
reality, fundamental, 37–44
Realpolitik, 108
realpolitische theory, 63
reason of state, 57, 105, 108, 128
rebellion, vs. war, 6
"Rebuilding America's Defenses," 98n8
recession, of 2008, 103
reciprocity, and nuclear weapons, 85n5
reconciliation, 3–5, 13, 14n16
    and the history of grace, 27–36
redemption
    and Christ, 6–8
    and the history of grace, 29
    and preservation, 8–10, 54–56
    and suffering, 49–51
relationships, international, 110–11, 117
"resort" criterion, 141
responsibility, of the leadership office, 115
restlessness, 38, 39n1, 48, 51, 136
retribution, and war, 46–48
revelation, 45
righteousness, of Noah, 52–53
rogue states, 80, 94–95, 102–4, 107, 116
role, in international relationships, 110–11
Roman Empire, 6, 29, 136
Roosevelt, Franklin, 76
Ross, Dennis, 73n6
"rule sets," and the civilization of power, 92–94
Runyon, Theodore, 1n1

salvation, historical, 62, 65
sanctification, and reconciliation, 32
Saudi Arabia, 4, 87
Schlesinger, James, 78n10
security, and peace, 151–52
sin
    and the order of preservation, 8–10
    original, 39n2, 53–60
    and war's judgment, 46–51
societas, 89–91
society
    justice in, 134
    and the military, 78–79
    and suffering, 48–49
    vulnerability in, 124–25
solution, political vs. military, 74–75
South Korea, 87
sovereignty, national, 95–100, 104
Soviet Union, 15, 84–86, 102, 123n1, 129, 134, 142
Staatspolitik, 73n7
Stalin, Joseph, 134, 142
starting point, theological, 148–50
Stassen, Glenn H., 64
state, the
    and globalization, 93–94
    and the order of preservation, 9–10
    types of, 94–97
    and war, 13–15
statements on war and peace, 156–58
state system, 127–28
    vs. international, 102–18
stewardship, of the international system, 116–18
study of war, 1, 157–58
Sturzo, Luigi, 57
suffering in war, 48–50
superiority, moral, in war, 50–51
Syria, 15
system. *See* international system; state system

technology, of weapons, 129
terrorism, 86, 94, 98, 107
theology
    dogmatic, 2
    and justice, 138–39
    and just war ethic, 10–11, 145–46
    liberation, 1–2, 27n1
    political, 1–2

INDEX

vs. politics, 22–23
   as starting point, 148–50, 156–58
theory, political, 105
Thielicke, Helmut, 9n7, 55n5, 73n7
Thompson, Kenneth W., 85n5
Tillich, Paul, 16
Toynbee, Arnold, 39n1
transcendence, of human beings, 63
transformation, 4, 62
"tribal" identities, 43
truce, vs. reconciliation, 33–34
Truman, Harry, 77–78
trust, ethos of, 124–25
Turkey, 76–77, 87
Twain, Mark, 103
Tzu, Sun, 75n8

Ukraine, 15
"under God," 154
United Nations, 72, 87, 106–9
United States, 4, 33n5, 75–77, 83–87, 102, 106–9, 123n1, 129, 142
   as a modern state, 96–99
   office of, 112–15
unity
   as divine intention, 40–41
   vs. reconciliation, 34–35
   war's disruption of, 44

Vance, Cyrus, 78n10
Vatican Council II, and nuclear weapons, 85n5
Venezuela, 15
Versöhnung, etymology of, 35–36
vicarious suffering, 49–51
victory, definition of, 74–75

violence
   controlling, 95–97, 100
   logic of, 69–70, 79–80
   renouncing, 5–8
vocation, human. *See* care, of creation; image of God
Voegelin, Eric, 57
von Rad, Gerhard, 29n2
vulnerable, freedom to be, 90, 96–97, 121–32, 152

Waltz, Kenneth N., 39n2
war
   absolute vs. real, 18–19
   definition of, 13–15
   study of, 1, 157–58
Warrior, God as, 29
weapons, 129, 157. *See also* nuclear weapons
Weber, Theodore R., 1n1, 13, 48n3, 71n3, 97n7, 109n7, 112n10, 145n4
Wesley, Charles, 63
Wesley, John, 13, 31–32, 47n2
will, bondage of, 61
Wilson, Woodrow, 76, 142
wisdom, prudential
   in the international system, 116–18
   and justice, 136–38
Wolfers, Arnold, 63n10, 71
Woodward, Bob, 78n10
world, and God, 27–32
world opinion, 135

Yoder, John Howard, 8, 144

www.ingramcontent.com/pod-product-compliance
Lightning Source LLC
Chambersburg PA
CBHW030113170426

43198CB00009B/606